CROSSING DISCIPLINES

A GUIDE FOR COLLEGE WRITING AND BEYOND

Kendall Hunt
publishing company

EDITED BY
KEITH KOPKA

Cover image © Shutterstock.com

Kendall Hunt
publishing company

www.kendallhunt.com
Send all inquiries to:
4050 Westmark Drive
Dubuque, IA 52004-1840

Copyright © 2021 by Kendall Hunt Publishing Company

ISBN 978-1-7924-2233-1

All rights reserved. No part of this publication may be reproduced, stored in a retrieval system, or transmitted, in any form or by any means, electronic, mechanical, photocopying, recording, or otherwise, without the prior written permission of the copyright owner.

Published in the United States of America

Table of Contents

Chapter 1 Writing in College and Beyond 1

Chapter 2 Essay Writing Skills: More Than Just an Essay 9

Chapter 3 Writing in Public Speaking and Communications 21

Chapter 4 Writing for Science and Labs 37

Chapter 5 APA Formatting in Nursing and Psychology 55

Chapter 6 Writing as a Student Learning to Become a Teacher 69

Chapter 7 A Guide to Writing History Papers 87

Chapter 8 Grammar and Mechanics 103

Chapter 9 Writing in the Digital World 113

Chapter 1
Writing in College and Beyond

What Is College Writing?

"College" writing has very much become its own distinct marketing category of writing in recent years. The growing number of "college" writing textbooks, supplements, and courses are clear evidence of this. Through this marketing lens, "college" writing is often defined by the freshman writing block experience.

Most students at four-year colleges take two introductory writing classes during their freshman year that are meant to prepare them for the writing that they are going to do over the next 3 years in the classes that are more connected to their chosen majors (If you are reading this, you are probably enrolled in one right now!). This, in theory, is a good thing. These classes are important. They help many students achieve what they need to achieve. However, this standardized approach, as with all standardized approaches, is not without flaws.

Many times, after freshman year, students choose majors that don't require much writing, and they lose the skills that they've gained in their introductory writing block because they are not consistently asked to practice these skills. Other times, because of the introductory nature of these composition classes, the essential elements of the types of writing that a student might need in their specific field are not covered. Because of these flaws, introductory writing classes are often treated as an obstacle, something that must merely be "cleared" in order to move on to the "important" work of one's specific major.

This is an understandable perspective. It costs a lot of money to go to college, and it is important to spend one's time and money wisely. However, it is also important not to ignore how, writing, one of the most central parts of education, will continue to be essential long after the cap and gown.

This supplemental text is built on the premise that there is no specifically "college" writing, and the idea of having to "get through" introductory writing classes so that one can move on to a life in which writing is no longer needed is as absurd as the idea that one will no longer need to do addition or subtraction again after passing a math class. Sure, algebra might not come up daily, just like MLA format might not, but the fundamentals of math, just like the fundamentals of writing, are the core structures of not only our education system but also most jobs, as well as most of our societal functions.

Freshman composition classes do a good job of introducing students to the major types of writing that will be expected of them in college. However, there is still a limited amount of time in these classes and many things get left out of the curriculum. This supplemental text is an attempt to help reinforce fundamentals with an eye toward the specific needs of students as they move beyond the freshman writing block and into the courses that they are going to take in their specific fields.

The goal of this text is to be a useful writing guide across all 4 years of college and beyond. We wanted to create something that will be used heavily and be as helpful as possible to as many students as possible. However, we also wanted to create something lasting, something that can be kept on a shelf in your apartment or family home, something that is referenced in those important moments when writing is, all of a sudden, a part of your life again.

To this end, this supplement is focused on providing essential information about general writing practices as well as specific guidance across the many types of specialized writing that students are often faced with after the composition classroom.

Structure of this Text

1) **Writing in College and Beyond**
   - An introduction to the text
2) **More Than Just an Essay**
   - How essay writing skills translate to other fields of study, are transferrable, connect to critical thinking, and so on.
3) **Writing Public Speaking and Communications**
   - Writing to address audience, outlining speeches, generating main points, and so on.
4) **Writing for Science and Labs**
   - Research report formatting, science writing strategies, citations unique to different fields, and so on.
5) **APA Formatting in Nursing and Psychology**
   - Formatting, the technical elements of citation in the APA style sheet, and so on.
6) **Writing as a Student Learning to Become a Teacher**
   - Lesson plan composition, writing for tenure and promotion, communicating with students and parents, and so on.

7) **A Guide to Writing History Papers**
   -Writing guide for short essays, research essays, book reviews, annotated bibliographies, and the Chicago style sheet.
8) **Grammar, Mechanics, and MLA Formatting Guidelines**
   -Supplemental information on grammar and mechanics MLA formatting, and so on.
9) **Writing in the Digital World**
   -Rhetoric, audience, the conventions of style, ethics, and so on.

Why Writing?

There is no shortage of book introductions or writing center articles that attempt to explain to college students why writing is important. The goal of these articles is to sell the idea of writing as something that is indispensable in ways that you, the student, have failed to recognize. These articles mean well, but, frankly, I find them insulting to the intelligence of college students.

You all know that writing is important. You might not want to admit it because it might not be your best subject, or you find MLA formatting annoying (who doesn't!?), or you just don't like writing as much as you like biology or psychology. That's ok. The goal of this text is not to get you to suddenly love writing (if that's a byproduct all the better!). Instead, the goal of this text is to give you easy access to the elements of writing that are most valuable to you so that you may employ them to your advantage. Writing is a vocation and an artform. However, it is also a tool, and we often forget this more utilitarian function in favor of more romantic ideals of writing.

Romance is not what this supplement is about. Instead, think of this text as a toolbox. You don't always need to hang a picture, but you are glad you have your hammer and level tucked away in the hall closet when you do!

Another major element of the dialogue around college writing often has to do with the idea of critical thinking. In the freshman writing classroom students are often asked to think critically about a variety of subjects and then translate those thoughts into essays. This translation often takes the form of thesis statements, outlines, argumentative structure, mimeses, and so on. However, at the core of all of these structures is a much simpler goal.

Caught up in the minutiae, it is sometimes easy to forget that behind all of the pomp and circumstance of the writing classroom is the simple goal of generating critical thought and then being able to translate that thought in written form so that others are able to understand what you are thinking. When you break it down to this base level, the writing classroom and its importance beyond the walls of the university is not so complicated.

Every major, every career, every element of our lives require some amount of critical thinking, and I don't think that anyone would argue against the idea that the ability to communicate your thoughts to others is invaluable in our careers, as well as in our lives in general. Still, it is easy to forget that this is the ultimate goal for many of us who are learning and practicing our writing.

In fact, some of the most common practices in the writing classroom are also the things that make us forget this ultimate goal. Measuring one's ability to successfully communicate critical thought is much more subjective and intangible than measuring one's ability to follow the correct formatting guidelines or one's ability to use three literary elements in a thesis statement. Many of the forms that educators created to be able to more easily and tangibly assess critical thought in writing (5-paragraph essays, 3-point thesis statements, etc.) are actually often the things that are stifling the critical thinking that your teachers are looking for.

It is undeniable that these formulaic writing processes do have benefits. They make it easier for students to begin to learn the techniques of critical thinking and written communication. But at some point, instead of fostering unique critical thought, students find themselves writing, and even thinking, to fill these formats rather than communicating unique thoughts or ideas. Even as students grow as critical thinkers, and are asked to think critically in new ways, they are also simultaneously asked to force those critical thoughts into recognizable forms that might undermine them. It is the nature of the beast.

Now, it might seem counterintuitive for a supplemental text that has referred to itself as a "toolbox" to also be criticizing the dangers of formulaic critical thinking. Still, it is important to draw a distinction. The goal of this text is to help you find ways to best express your critical thoughts through writing in a variety of different academic and professional fields. However, the goal is not to force square pegs into round holes or make all critical thoughts fit formulaic ideas. Instead, the goal within this text is to provide you with the necessary tools, so that you may use them to confidently express your thoughts through writing in any way that is useful to you. Ultimately, we hope that these tools are able to help you find a balance between more technical, formulaic writing and true self-expression. There is a time and a place for each, but you should feel empowered to do both when you need to.

A Note About Genre

"Genre" is, basically, the category that the composition that you are working on falls into. To borrow from music, songs are general compositions, but each one often falls into a different, specific genre (punk, metal, R&B, classical, etc.). Ultimately, what you are going to be using this supplement for is to find a way to compose the best text possible within your specific field or genre.

What is important to note about the idea of genre is that it, like most things in our lives, is not an absolute. Instead, it is something that exists on a spectrum. Genre at once sets up boundaries and categories but also defies them in the same breath. Again, to use music as an example, I bet you can think of a song that draws from both pop and R&B to create a unique composition that is successful but also difficult to categorize. This is an important thing to keep in mind as you use this supplemental writing guide.

Just because the chapter that you are reading focuses on a type of writing that does not appear to immediately fit into your field of study, it doesn't mean that the writing elements of that other field are not useful to the ways in which you compose your writing. In many ways, like musical genres, these are artificial categories. For example, just because you might primarily be composing formal lesson plans as an education major, and in your future work as an educator, it doesn't mean that the writing skills that are outlined in the public speaking chapter will not be important to you in the future. There will be many opportunities in your career as an educator to employ these skills in your written communication that will be to your advantage: dealing with parents, emailing students, conversing with colleagues, and so on.

All of this is to say, do not ignore the information that is presented to you in the chapters that are not specifically addressed to your field. This is a cross-curricular text, and all of the chapters are in conversation with each other. All you need to do is decide what type of writing is best for that *rhetorical situation* that you are in.

Rhetoric is linked to your ability to write and communicate effectively and with purpose. It is the way in which you connect with you audience. A rhetorical situation is the context in which you are writing. For example, you are going to write a different type of email to your professor than to your friend from home. One is going to be much more formal than the other. Being able to identify these rhetorical situations so that you can employ the best strategies contained in this supplement is going to be key to your growth as an effective writer both in and out of the academic setting. In order to identify any rhetorical situation you need to ask yourself two important questions:

To whom am I writing?
Why am I writing?

By answering these two questions you are taking into consideration two of the most important elements of rhetoric: purpose and audience.

We already outlined why audience is important through the example of the email composition. But there are a few other questions you can ask yourself to make sure that you are identifying the correct rhetorical situation and relating to your audience in the best way possible:

Why does my audience care about the information that I'm presenting?
What is the demographic of my audience (age, religion, gender, ethnicity, etc.)?
What are the values of my audience?
What is the education level of my audience?

By answering these questions, you will be able to identify the rhetorical situation as it relates to the people that you are writing for. Once you have figured out the "who," the next step is to understand "why" you are writing. It's not enough just to say, "because the writing was assigned to me." Remember, someday soon you are going to be asked to write for your career, and there will be no "assignments," just things that need to be done. You can begin to identify why you are writing by asking yourself the following:

What do I want to communicate?
What do I want my audience to believe?
Is what I'm writing about controversial or difficult for my audience?
Is what I'm communicating important?

Answering these questions allows you to see how your subject and your audience are interrelated. For example, someday you might be tasked with delivering bad news in an office-wide memo. You will need to decide how to deliver this news, and by asking yourself the questions above you can decide the best tactic for the ultimate goal of your communication. For example, you might decide to sugarcoat the bad news you need to deliver because, ultimately, your goal is to boost morale, or you might decide to be forceful and upsetting in your delivery so that your audience believes that their jobs are on the line. It all depends on the situation, but, either way, the use of rhetoric branches across all types of writing, and it is used in all academic and career settings.

When you are composing in a specific genre and considering audience and purpose it is also important to take into account the "medium" of your composition. "Medium" is another word for the delivery mode of your composition, and it influences the ways in which your audience will experience your message. Some of the most common mediums are: textual, visual, and audio. However, within the textual medium there are also different "modes." For example, you could have digital text or printed textual. The same goes for visual modes (paintings, digital graphics, etc.) and audio modes (speeches, music, etc.). If we relate this back to the idea of "genre," a mode is like a "sub-genre" of the medium that you are using to deliver your composition.

It is important to pay attention to these different delivery systems because each of them will have an impact on how you are delivering your message to your audience. In other words, the medium that you are working with has its own conventions that must be considered in addition to the conventions of the genre in which you are composing. When all of these factors come together successfully, you will be able to successfully compose the best piece of writing for your audience in the best medium or mode for the information that you are attempting to deliver.

A Note about Writing and Confidence

Lastly, I just want to take a brief moment before you dive into the contents of this book to point out that there are parts of it that will, inevitably, challenge you. You are still learning how to write, and there are going to be moments of frustration and doubt along the way. Do not give up. Many students, by the time they arrive at college, have already decided whether or not they are a "good" writer, or, even worse, they've had that decision made for them by some sort of authority figure.

As you read this text, remember, writing is not about "good" or "bad." Instead, it is about how successfully you are able to use writing to achieve the goals that you are hoping to accomplish in your life. In this sense, you are always able to grow as a writer, and, hopefully, by using this supplemental text, you will be able to approach writing in new ways and with new and specific purpose.

Do not be intimidated by the written word. It is something that you are going to be using for the rest of your life in one capacity or another, so it is important to build a healthy working relationship with it. Remember, this book is filled with tools, and we are going to learn how to use them together.

Chapter 2
Essay Writing Skills: More Than Just an Essay

Introduction

Did you ever attend a football game or go to a movie where you said at the end, "This just was not worth the price I paid." Most people have probably had this experience, and it is a disappointing one. You remember the feeling it evoked, and it isn't a positive one. You do not want to have others, or yourself, judge your writing in that fashion.

Most students have had ample writing assignments in their elementary and high school career. Some have been enticing; many were not so exciting. In fact, let's admit it, some assignments were downright boring. These are often the kinds of assignments that students will respond to by saying, "I do not know what to write about or even where to start."

This chapter will enable you to sort out what you need to know to write a really good essay. Now understand, not all topics will be on your top 10 list of interests. However, that will not prohibit you from completing an essay of which you can be proud.

If your professor allows you to choose a topic, then select something that interests you. You will usually do a much better job if you are researching a topic that is of importance to you. If you are assigned a topic, read up on it and discover an aspect of it that you can delve into. Even if it is a topic that you have never heard of, researching it will often turn up a facet of it that appeals to you or at least something that can be developed. Suppose you were assigned a paper to write on a composer. Knowing very little about composers, the first step might be to begin to research the list given to the class. Perhaps in your research you read a sentence comparing a composer to the writer Chaucer. You remember Chaucer from your high school English class, so you make a list of characteristics about this writer and then compare that list to what you have learned about the composer and his work, and before you know it you are on your way to constructing a clear and well-written essay.

Anyone can do this. It all begins with the confidence and the knowledge of where to begin making connections and the process you need to follow in order to turn the connections you've made into a well-organized essay.

Still, before you begin anything, you need to know the basics of writing. In order to convey your ideas to the world or to your classmates, you need to be able to write in good, standard English. No one is going to continue reading your essay if the first three lines contain several spelling and/or grammatical errors. There is an argument to be made that in our growing digital world, where written communication is often in shorthand, our English skills have gotten less and less use. However, as a college student, you are tasked with being able to transition from your daily communications to academic communications and vice versa.

Writing is a life-long skill that no one else can acquire for you but yourself. Your work will be different from anyone else's, and the need to hear your voice is essential. However, it is also a skill that everyone is capable of acquiring with a little practice. So, let's get started.

Overview of Chapter:

I. Introduction
II. The Basics
   A. Imitation Is the Sincerest Form of Flattery
   B. Brainstorming
   C. Outlining and Research
      1. Eating Disorders in Teenage Women
   D. Thesis Statement
   E. Arguable Theses versus Statements of Fact
   F. Specificity in Your Thesis
   G. Introduction and Hook
   H. Argument and Transitions
   I. Conclusion
III. Types of Essays
   J. Critical Analysis Essay
   K. Exploratory Essay
   L. Reaction–Response Essay
   M. Narrative Essay
   N. Argumentative Essay

©sheff/Shutterstock.com

The Basics

If you are learning to play baseball or play the drums, you would need to have gotten the inspiration to do so from another source. Perhaps you have been to a major league baseball game, and you just know that being a catcher is the position you want to play. Or you may have gone to a concert and fell in love with the sound of the drums. In your head, you can see yourself catching that ball or playing that beat, time and again. You are so sure of your ability that it is as if you have that movie playing over and over in your mind. The tape never gets old. So, you begin to plan to make this aspiration a reality.

Imitation Is the Sincerest Form of Flattery

Your first step in this plan is to learn the rules of the skills that you are trying to gain and then practice them. If you are learning to play baseball, for example, you might join a team with a skilled coach to help you practice and guide you on your way, and it is a safe bet to say that if you enjoy what you are doing, or you like your coach, then you will practice more. The same method applies to writing. Reading is your "coach" in this regard. Investigate how other authors craft their material. Figure out which authors you like best and then analyze their work. The steps they take to convey their message may seem seamless to you as a reader, but it has taken much time and effort on their part to achieve that goal. The very fact that you do not notice any splits in their seams is an indication of just how well they have performed their task. If you finish reading a piece and say to yourself, "Wow! That was really well-written," or "I wish I had written that myself" then you know that this is good material.

You do not necessarily have to read William Shakespeare or William Faulkner to understand this point (even though they are great authors). Modern writers such as Stephen King, Jodi Picoult, or J.K. Rowling may be better to your liking. You may have a favorite sports writer or movie critic who can get the point across and have you look forward to reading their work. Each writer can display a different perspective or present a challenge for you to unlock the details that are to follow.

> **Exercise:**
> Pick a piece of writing that you admire. This could be a book or an article, or it could be a short story or a poem. Compose a paragraph of at least 300 words discussing and analyzing the reasons why you are drawn to this piece of writing. Ask yourself: What about this writing that makes me like it? Are there certain elements of the composition (tone, diction, form, image, etc.) that make this piece of writing more enjoyable to you? How could you apply some of these tactics to your own academic writing?

Brainstorming

Brainstorming is your next line of defense. When you begin a piece of writing, your ideas may be all over the place. Do not worry; this is natural. Start to jot down your ideas and then cluster them together. You do not need to be fussy about what form they take. Group similar ideas together and then start branching out. You will find that the more you think about your ideas, the clearer they will become. This visual representation is akin to the diagram that a football coach shares with the players during practice. The players have their input and then plays begin to gel. Likewise, you will want to share your brainstorming thoughts with others and get their take on what you are about to do. Peer editing is a wonderful way to collaborate and to have your concepts validated. This all may take some time, so be willing to put the time into it. If possible, try to go back to your brainstorming a day later and unearth your own creativity.

> **Exercise:**
> Brainstorming can take many forms, but it is important that we practice it in order to build our confidence in our brainstorming skills. Think about the very general topic of "healthcare." By yourself or in a group, brainstorm five different and specific potential essay topics that you could write about this topic.

Outlining and Research

Once you have named your ideas, structure them into an outline. The outline is a vital piece of the writing process. It is your personal GPS for where you are going with your essay. You will want to include your ideas from your brainstorming activity and refine them in such a way that they form a cohesive whole. The outline helps you avoid going into a dead end and keeps you on the straight and narrow. However, it does not have to be set in stone. If you find a new pathway while composing your essay, you can adjust your outline to give you the freedom of fluidity in your work. At its best, your outline should provide the structure you need to forge ahead with your research.

As with each part of your essay, do not be afraid to make changes. Your thoughts may evolve on some items. You will detect information that may tweak your original concept, your research may shed light on a different angle of your essay, and your talking to a professional person may enable you to view ideas from a different lens. Your essay is a living, breathing work that is created by you—the writer. It is not a stagnant structure that is completed because it has to be done just for a grade. Here is an example of an outline for an essay about Frederick Douglas:

Eating Disorders in Teenage Women

Thesis: This study of anorexia examines the effect of personal, familial, and culture/media on the young woman experiencing this disorder.

I. Introduction
   A. Define anorexia
   B. Population that it affects
   C. The typical young woman as an anorectic
II. Personal
   A. Concept of invisibility
   B. Weight: actual and perceived
   C. Self-control and perfectionism
III. Familial
   A. Relationship with father and other male figures
   B. Relationship with mother and other female figures
   C. Relationship with siblings and friends
IV. Media/Culture
   A. Celebrities
   B. Sports figures

    C. Coaches and other authority figures
    D. Advertisements
V. Conclusion
    A. Treatment
    B. The day-to-day struggle
    C. Future challenges

Take your outline in hand and run, do not walk, to the library. Your skill at texting and downloading all types of information is probably first rate; however, academic databases are the gold standard for writing papers. Your librarian can assist you in finding peer-review sources for your topic. These works are published by credible academic institutions and will make the argument in your essay. By using your outline as a guide, you should be able to uncover vital information. Keep in mind that you will want to stay within the 5- to 7-year range for information with the exception being foundational sources. This will keep your paper current and up to date.

> **Exercise:**
> Choose one of the topics that you brainstormed in the previous exercise. By yourself or with a group, spend some time researching the topic. Next, compose an outline for a potential paper that you might want to write about the subject.

Thesis Statement

Your thesis is the ultimate guide for your essay. A strong thesis will allow you to compose a strong essay, but a weak thesis will leave your readers confused about your topic. There are many different ways to approach thesis writing depending on the subject and the purpose of your essay, but there are some basic elements of thesis composition that are true across the board.

Arguable Theses versus Statements of Fact

A statement of fact is a statement that cannot be argued—at least not logically. For example, a clear statement of fact would be: *water is needed for human survival.*

Students often craft a thesis around a statement of fact when they are having a difficult time connecting with an essay topic. Statements of fact can seem like an alluring place to begin a thesis because the argument seems to make itself. However, this will not help you write a clear essay in your body paragraphs. If the argument makes itself, you have no content for the body of the essay.

Instead of focusing on a statement of fact in a thesis you should instead focus on a statement that is **arguable.** If you find yourself leaning toward a statement of fact it is important to change that statement so that you are able to create an argument. Look at the following statements of fact and consider the differences in their corresponding arguable thesis versions.

Statement of fact: Excessive alcohol consumption causes health problems
Arguable thesis: The government should ban the sale of alcoholic beverages

Statement of fact: There is violence in movies

Arguable thesis: Violence in movies has a negative effect on viewers and has led to more violent actions by people in American culture

Specificity in Your Thesis

Another common issue that students often encounter when they are beginning to write a thesis statement for their essay is that their ideas are often too general for the composition of a clear and direct thesis.

A specific thesis is necessary because it allows you to focus your writing in your essay. If a topic is too large you won't be able to cover it all in your essay, and your readers will be left with large questions about the argument you are making or the idea that you are informing them about. For example, writing an essay on the topic of education is too broad. There are so many topics that could be included in this essay: funding, necessity, charter schools, parental involvement, teacher certification, and the list goes on. However, if you narrow that topic from education to distance education you have taken an important step toward successful thesis composition. This topic is narrower, and you are able to perhaps find three or four specific subtopics within the realm of distance education to include in your arguable thesis. Consider the following thesis on the topic of distance education:

Distance education is the future of American higher ed because it is more affordable for students, is adaptable to a variety of learning styles, and provides more opportunities for students to learn safely.

Notice how the thesis takes the narrower topic of distance learning and connects it to even more specific elements of argument within the thesis.

> **Exercise**
> Compose thesis statements for the following narrowed topics:
>
> | General Topic | Narrower Topic Thesis Statement |
> |---|---|
> | 1. communication | _____ the difference in people's voices |
> | 2. work | _____ paid vacation time |
> | 3. dishonesty | _____ cheating in sports |
> | 4. community | _____ volunteerism |
> | 5. television | _____ reality shows |
> | 6. relationships | _____ fathers and sons |
> | 7. newspapers | _____ college newspapers |
> | 8. family | _____ eating together |
> | 9. criminal justice | _____ treatment of inmates |

Introduction and Hook

Once you have your thesis and your outline, it is time to stop reading and to start writing. You need to "hook" your reader into wanting to read your essay. Of course, your professor has no choice but to read it, but it would be so much more pleasant if the introduction lured him or her into wanting to read what you wrote.

Edgar Allan Poe began his short story, "The Cask of Amontillado" with the sentence, "The thousand injuries of Fortunato I had borne as I best could, but when he ventured upon insult, I vowed revenge." Kate Chopin introduces her "Story of an Hour" with, "Knowing that Mrs. Mallard was afflicted with a heart trouble, great care was taken to break to her as gently as possible the news of her husband's death." What exciting ways to begin a work! How could one not want to know what is to follow! Feel free to use an anecdote, statistics, an awesome quote—anything that will draw your reader into reading your paper.

You will want to do similarly with your introduction. Let your audience know how and why you are going to write about this topic. Inform the reader of your major points and end your introduction with your thesis statement. This should be your main position on your topic and one that you will enhance throughout your paper. Your thesis is the compass point for your paper. By the end of the paper, you should have been able to have proven your thesis with evidence to support it.

Argument and Transitions

"Let's start at the very beginning; a very good place to start." So begin the words from the song "Do Re, Mi." Yet with writing, you may not feel as comfortable writing the beginning first. That is not a problem. If you have your outline and thesis completed, then you know what has to be done. When you are composing your essay, choose that section with which you are most comfortable.

As you get into the body of your paper, be sure that you are focused. Keep that thesis statement in the forefront of your mind. Know what type of essay you are writing. A critical-analysis essay is different from a narrative essay. Your audience must be considered as well as your tone.

Your argument must be a blend of your ideas supported by research. If either one is not balanced properly, your paper becomes just that—a piece of paper. The three essentials to be considered are: ethos, logos, and pathos.

Ethos: You become the master of your work. You design the thesis and outline and find academic voices to support them. You need to convince your audience that you know what you are writing about on this issue.

Logos: Your argument must make sense. That might seem obvious, but it is not always so. Do not let anyone let the air out of your essay by finding one statement that does not add up. Once that happens, no one is going to trust the rest of your work.

Pathos: You must appeal to your audience. Make them want more as you entice them onto your path of knowledge. (Have them follow the Yellow Brick Road so they can see the Wizard.)

Remember, while stating your side of the argument using ethos, pathos, and logos, do not neglect the opposing viewpoint. Provide credible sources for the other side. Just be sure to build up your opinion with more than enough support so you leave the reader with no doubt where your stance lies.

Follow your outline. If you do not have enough support for a particular point, you need to go back and do further research. Be sure all correct citations are used (see Chapter 7). You do not want to cross the boundary into plagiarism. (Plagiarism is the use of another's language, thoughts, ideas, or expressions as your own original work.) This can result in an automatic failure and possible further difficulty for the student.

Check and double-check spelling, grammar, and mechanics (see Chapter 9). These are things that can detract from your paper. They are easily fixable, and they just take a little extra bit of effort to correct. After a *ho-hum* introduction, the misuse of grammar and correct usage rules will ensure that a professor is underwhelmed with your paper.

Use transitional words, phrases, and sentences to segue from one main topic to the next. Everyone knows that *The Star Spangled Banner* is played at the beginning of a baseball game and then the first inning starts. Likewise, the seventh inning stretch is a time to get up, move around, and get ready for the final two innings.

50 Transitional Words and Phrases

absolutely	equally	never
above all	especially	nevertheless
additionally	finally	not only … but also
along with	for example	obviously
also	for instance	overall
alternatively	for this reason	similarly
as a consequence	furthermore	therefore
as a result of	generally	thus
besides	hence	to clarify
because of	importantly	to put it differently
clearly	in addition	undoubtedly
conversely	in conclusion	unless
consequently	in fact	unquestionably
correspondingly	in order to	without a doubt
definitely	in particular	
desperate	moreover	
due to	namely	

Conclusion

When you began your essay, you let your audience know what you intended to tell them. In the body, you presented your facts and support. In the conclusion you will tell the reader what you told them. Restate your thesis (in a different way than in the introduction). Summarize your important points and end with a strong impression that the reader can remember as he or she walks away from your paper. This is often achieved by reminding your audience of the importance of your topic in relationship to the larger world outside of your essay.

Before you turn your paper in to your professor, take time to reread what you have written. Record it and play it back for yourself or read the essay out loud to yourself or a friend. This practice will help you catch many of the grammatical/syntactical mistakes you might have overlooked while rereading. If you don't feel comfortable sharing with a friend, more than likely, there is a tutoring center available to you at your school. Of course, you will need to complete your paper ahead of time in order to do this. The people in the centers are usually more than willing to help you and, better yet, their services are free. So you want to take advantage of this valuable resource.

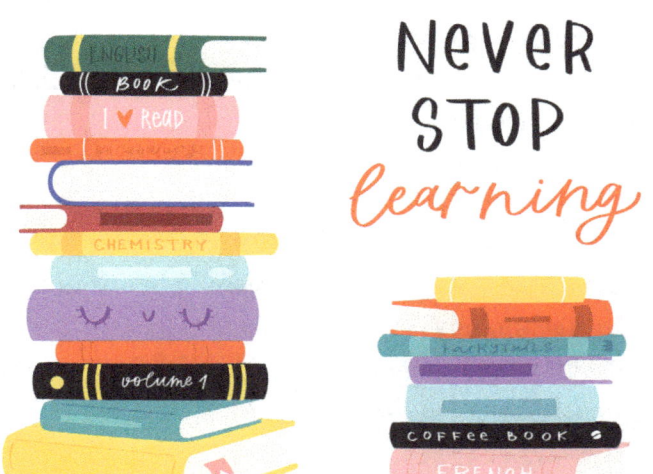

Remember, writing is a learning process. By reviewing your professor's remarks when you receive your paper back, you can learn more about their expectations and prepare yourself to compose an even better essay for your next assignment. If you do not understand the comments or corrections that your professor has made, make an appointment to meet with them so you can understand the remarks more fully.

Types of Essays

What follows is a quick synopsis of different types of essays that can be used in many areas of study. Peruse the PENS method: **P**urpose, **E**ssential points, **N**otes for writing, and **S**uggested topics, when you decide on which type of essay you will be writing.

For essays in specific academic disciplines, refer to: Chapter 3 (Business, Public Speaking, and Communications); Chapter 4 (Science); Chapter 5 (Nursing and Psychology); Chapter 6 (Primary and Secondary Education).

Critical Analysis Essay

Purpose: To evaluate a work (literary, movie, art) and present it to your audience in an understandable way.

Essential points: Decipher the writer's thesis and goals. If necessary, research some angles that are not clear to you.

Notes for writing: Be focused on your topic. Evaluate its strengths and weaknesses. Use examples from the text to support your ideas.

Suggested topics:

1. Making the world more "*green*" and "*solar*"
2. Street art and graffiti
3. Multicultural identity
4. Changing gender roles
5. Examine a novel based on a comic book series

Exploratory Essay

Purpose: To focus on a specific problem, give a detailed explanation, and offer a possible solution

Essential points: A need to research thoroughly and present those points in the body of your paper. Stay structured.

Notes for writing: Be highly informative in your main points. Do not take sides on the issue. Be objective.

Suggested topics:

1. Effects of early marriage
2. Use of DNA and gene screening in criminal cases
3. Technology: solution or danger to society
4. Effect of food allergies
5. China as a global superpower

Reaction–Response Essay

Purpose: To explain a personal reaction to a topic

Essential points: Do not evaluate the data objectively; explain your subjective viewpoint.

Notes for writing: Present a strong thesis statement to convince the reader of your perception. Follow your main points in this regard.

Suggested Topics:

1. Families must be responsible for the behavior of their children.
2. How much can noise pollution affect people?
3. Is it a good idea to arm teachers?
4. Should the United States follow the U.K. *custom year of gap* between high school and college?
5. Hidden criminality: sexual assault against women

Narrative Essay

Purpose: Tell a story. It can be experiential, anecdotal, or personal.

Essential points: Rely on concrete, sensory details. Use vivid and colorful language.

Notes for writing: Write in the first person. Be clear and concise. Include all the parts of a story. Concentrate on a central point or motif.

Suggested topics:

1. Suffering an injury
2. A time you experienced rejection.
3. A difficult decision you had to make.
4. A time you experienced a historic event.
5. An experience that was hard but ended up being worth it.

Argumentative Essay

Purpose: To investigate a topic; collect, generate, and evaluate evidence; establish a position on the topic in a concise manner.

Essential points: Provide a clear, concise thesis statement. Should be thought-provoking. Research is essential. Be logical and cohesive.

Notes for writing: Evidence must be in the body paragraphs. Show differing opinions.

Conclusion must be based on evidence. Do not simply restate your thesis.

Suggested topics:

1. Is the U.S. election process fair?
2. Should men be allowed paternity leave from work?
3. Should animals be used for research?
4. Should companies market to children?
5. Do violent video games cause behavior problems?

Many of these essays can be used for the various disciplines you will encounter in your collegiate academic career. Your understanding of the issues concerned will connect to your critical thinking skills. Planning your essay is essential to producing a good work. Do not just sit down and think you will "knock this out of the park."

Upon entering the workforce or furthering your education, you will be faced with completing different assignments. Having a plan will lead you to have a clear path to follow in writing reports, briefs, business plans, lesson plans, memos, letters, and other work-related materials.

Remember your writing is *you*. Make it the best *you* possible.

> **Final Exercise: Composing your Essay**
>
> Using what you have learned in this chapter it is now time to bring together all of the essay writing elements that we have discussed to model an essay from concept to the point of composition. Using either a topic that you brainstormed or a topic provided to you by your teacher, please spend time brainstorming around your topic. Next, compose an outline and a thesis for your topic. After you have a thesis and an outline, please compose the opening and concluding paragraphs of your essay.

Chapter 3
Writing in Public Speaking and Communications

Introduction

While there will be a few similarities between your writing in ENGL-101/102 and in ENGL-115, there is one key difference that can make or break your success in your Public Speaking course: that is, your ability to **draft** and **revise** an **outline.** This chapter will familiarize you with the key terms around outlining and offer tips on how to use best practices when constructing your outlines. This chapter will serve as the bridge between your textbook and the outlines you will be generating for this class. You should consult this chapter before you begin your first speech outline draft.

Writing for Public Speaking

Overview of Chapter:

I. Introduction
II. Writing for public Speaking
   A. First thing's (Not always) First: Identifying Your Speech's Goal
   B. Before the Thesis: Generating Your Main Points
III. Sample Outline
   C. A Much-Needed Change for Students
      1. Introduction
      2. Body
      3. Conclusion
      4. Research Notes
IV. Outline Template
   D. Title
      1. Introduction
      2. Body
      3. Conclusion
      4. Research Notes
V. Conclusion with Sample Exercises

First Thing's (Not Always) First: Identifying Your Speech's Goal

Like the **thesis statements** you compose in ENGL-101/102, or that you may have written for English papers in high school, your **Public Speaking thesis** (alternately referred to in textbooks as a "specific purpose statement" or "central idea") appears at the end of your introduction and **previews** or summarizes the main points you will cover in the speech, while also making the goal of the speech clear to your audience. In a **Creative Speech**, your thesis will simply involve articulating your speech's goal—whether that's teaching your audience how to knit or using a story from your childhood to toast your sibling at their wedding. In an **Informative Speech,** your thesis will involve concisely previewing your main points, while also making clear why you believe your topic is important. In a **Persuasive Speech**, you will want to make your stance on your topic clear, while previewing the main points you will present to the audience in an attempt to bring them closer to your thinking on the issue at hand.

For the purposes of ENGL-115 at Holy Family University, we will refer to the end of your introduction as your **thesis statement,** but if you go on to study Communications further, you may encounter terms like "central idea" or "specific purpose statement" in reference to the preview of your main points and the articulation of the goals of your speech.

Before the Thesis: Generating Your Main Points

Students often ask us, "What should I say in my thesis statement?" To which we reply, "Well, that depends on what you want to talk about in the body of your speech!" Everyone's writing process is a little bit different; while some students benefit from articulating their thesis first, most students tend to first map out their **main points** as a way of seeing what they plan on saying and in what order. The latter is also the method that educators recommend.

Start by jotting down what you already know about a given topic, as well as what you are interested in researching further. That will help you to see what you need to look for as you conduct your research and will point you toward your speech's eventual main points. This process of freewriting, and of following the threads of your interests to lead you to research and further writing, is referred to as **drafting.**

Here are some important things to know about main points and **outlining**, mapped out in the same outline structure your instructor will expect of your own written speeches (parts of the outline are labeled in italics):

I. *Main Point:* Use Google Docs or Microsoft Word to organize your speech in outline format (just like these very instructions are formatted). Please do not use Pages, as that application is not compatible with all operating systems.
   a. *Sub-point:* Use an indented outline system (also called "Multilevel List" in Microsoft Word) to distinguish main points, sub-points, and sub-sub points.
   b. *Sub-point:* A **sub-point** belongs under a given main point if it provides more detail about the same topic as that main point. For example, in this outline, "Sub-point a" relates to "Main Point I" by continuing to describe outline formats, but it also goes a step further by defining indented outline systems. That makes it a Sub-point of this Main Point.
      i. *Sub-sub-point:* A **sub-sub-point** belongs under a sub-point if it provides more detail about the same topic as that sub-point. Think of it this way: Every time you elaborate on a point, you want to click "enter" and "tab/indent," so that you can see how much you have to say about a certain aspect of your topic.
   c. *Sub-point:* In contrast, if your next "point" moves on to another aspect of the main point, it is a sub-point, not a sub-sub-point.
   d. *Sub-point:* You can toggle your indents back and forth by using the "Increase Indent" or "Decrease Indent" buttons, which should appear with left- and right-facing arrows in your Word menu bar.

e. *Sub-point*: If this seems confusing now, don't worry. We'll look at a sample outline soon, which should help to clarify these distinctions.
      i. *Sub-sub-point*: Notice as this outline continues—and in the sample outline—that the labels of *"Main Point, "Sub-point,"* and *"Sub-sub-point"* fall out as we progress. Similarly, you will also be expected to rely on the indented outline system, rather than writing out the phrase *"Main Point"* next to your **topic sentences**.
II. Unlike the three-pronged thesis statements you may have often written for English papers in high school, your speeches will not always have three main points.
   a. Some topics may only require two main points, while some may require four or five.
   b. The number of main points in a speech depends on the number of your topic's main features on which you intend to focus.
      i. For example, a speech focused on informing your audience about bees might have four main points: the hive, the queen, pollination, and extinction.
         1. The sample speech could also be organized with a narrower lens, focusing on the declining population of bees. It will be up to you to determine the **scope** of your speech—that is, how much about the topic you will be able to include, given the time limit.
      ii. On the other hand, a speech focused on persuading your audience to recycle might have two main points: the harmful impact of single-use plastics on the environment, and how to obtain a recycle bin in order to begin recycling.
III. You will want to write the following parts of your outline in full sentences:
   a. **Hook**: Your outline's first, biggest, and most creative point, where you get your audience's attention!
   b. **Thesis**: Your outline's most important point, where you preview your main points and tell us about the goal of your speech.
   c. **Main Points/Connectives**: We advise writing your main points as full sentences, so that you remember which three or four "big" topics you need to cover before you leave the stage.
      i. Often, your topic sentence will also serve as a transition between two main points, making it a connective: a clear articulation of what point you just covered and what point you are about to cover next.
   d. **Oral Citations**: When you are using quotations from your research, you will want to write down a substantial portion of original material (so that you deliver the quote accurately) *and* you will want to attribute that material.
      i. Basically, if you're going to use someone else's words, tell us where those words are coming from and that they are someone else's.
      ii. Rules around plagiarism in Public Speaking differ slightly from in your other English courses. Because it's more important to your teacher that you get up in front of your peers and confidently deliver an informed speech, we will not detract points if you planned to include an oral citation but forgot to do so when you delivered the speech itself.
         1. This is also why we ask you to keep Research Notes, jotting down everything you learned from a given resource, and making sure your notes also follow an indented outline system. You will see a sample Research Notes page in the next section.

2. Consider oral citations and research notes to be proof to your teacher that you had good intentions and included quotes in your research and speech; they are a failsafe in the event that you forget to orally cite your quotes when it comes time to deliver in front of your peers.
   e. **Sendoff:** Your speech's final point; this is the memorable final sentence of your speech, so it is important to remember to say it, and say it well!
IV. In contrast, there is no need to write the following in full sentences:
   a. Sub-points
   b. Sub-sub-points
      i. Sub-points and sub-sub-points make up the bulk of your research on a given topic, so they comprise most of your outline's content.
      ii. Rather than write out word-for-word what you plan on saying, sub-points are good places to jot down phrases as reminders of what you want to bring up in relation to a given main point.
      iii. The same goes for sub-sub-points. You may want to connect those phrases with an → or ... or –, as you'll see in the sample below. The rule of thumb for sub- and sub-sub-points is to make sure that you aren't writing full sentences but that you instead *only give yourself as much text as you need in order to remember what you plan to say*.
   c. Summary of main points in conclusion
      i. You should know the main concepts, or points, of your speech by heart—or at least well enough to remind us what we just heard you cover in your speech!
V. Here's one final reminder before you read a sample speech outline and review the assignment template: *start by writing the body of the speech first*.
   a. Second, write your introduction, based on what you have written in your main points.
      i. Remember, you need to see *what* you're going to say in the speech before you can introduce your audience to the speech's contents!
   b. Finally, draft your conclusion, making sure that it refers in some way to your introduction. This might occur by way of repetition of your main points, or you might want your sendoff to refer back to your hook. You will learn new strategies for creatively concluding as the semester progresses.
   c. Your very last step before submitting *both* your outline draft and outline revision is to **revise** the outline—edit as you reread your work, both on the level of grammar and syntax and on the level of broader organizational issues and speech length. Ultimately, you should revise your speech with a critical eye toward how well the speech seems to flow.
      i. In all likelihood, you will not be able to successfully revise your speech if you do not record yourself delivering your outline draft.

ii. Just like with the drafting process itself, you need to *hear* what you're actually going to say in order to critically review it and make changes.
iii. This is why you are assigned a **video draft** for each speech.

Sample Outline

A Much-Needed Change for Students

Introduction

I. As students, we have lived through the terrors of waking up early and experiencing exhaustion throughout our middle and high school days.
II. A later start time for schools would eliminate the exhaustion for students. *(PAUSE!)*
III. According to questionnaire, 70% agreed K-12 schools should start later.
IV. I went to a school far from where I reside—had to wake up early—struggled with exhaustion.
V. Today, I am here to show you the effects of an early start time, how to efficiently advocate for a change in this policy, and the positive benefits of a later start time for students.

PAUSE! BREATHE!

Body

I. Main Point 1: What students go through daily because of the lack of sleep is absurd.
  A. Middle schools start around 8:00 a.m.; high schools around 7:30 a.m.
    a. Too early to begin learning, according to the American Academy of Pediatrics, the American Medical Association, and the American Academy of Sleep Medicine *(PAUSE)*
    b. Survey—Youth Risk Behavior—2015—57% middle schoolers—72% high schoolers—did not—8–10 hours
  B. Adults perceive a stereotype that kids do not receive enough sleep because they are up late on their phones
    1. Scientifically not true *(PAUSE)*
    2. Circadian rhythm—24-hour cycle—tired/awake—day/night
      a. Puberty—changes—rhythm
      b. UCLA Health states that before puberty, your circadian rhythm makes you tired around 8:00–9:00 p.m., and after puberty, around 10:00–11:00 p.m., hence why we stay up later as we get older
        (a) 2011 sleep poll—12th grade—6.9 hours—compared—8.4 hours—6th grade—freighting! *(PAUSE)*
        (b) Rhythm changes—school start time—does not
  C. Result—many students suffer from sleep deprivation
    1. According to the National Sleep Foundation, 70% of adolescents sleep less than 8 hours each night
    2. Lack—sleep—impact—students
      a. Stanford Medical—depression—anxiety—lack of concentration—schools—sports—work—poor grades—suicide—concerning problem

II. Main Point 2: Early start time for schools is negatively impacting students. Change is absolutely necessary to benefit the student's health, sleep, and education, but how?
   A. To be realistic, start locally in Bucks County—thirteen school districts—most impactful
   B. First—ask—when—advocate—policy?
      1. Before—school—year—advocate for change ***(PAUSE!)***
   C. Who—involved?
      1. Advocates—students—parents—teachers—administrators—doctors ***(BREATHE!)***
   D. Process for change—begins with principal
      1. Expressing—importance—work—benefit—students—important—final decision
         a. Persuading—principal—next step—School Committee—system wide—outside of Bucks County ***(PAUSE! GESTURE!)***
   E. Schools—46 states—have advocated—changed time
      1. Jilly Dos Santos—fought—later time—hard time with waking up
         a. Strong support—social media—changed time—7:20 a.m.—8:55 a.m.
         b. Superintendent—suspensions dropped 1,000—graduation rose 82% to 90%—incredible!

PAUSE! INFLECTIONS! KEEP GOING!

III. Main Point 3: How would this policy benefit students?
   A. Would be beneficial—students in 270 Bucks County schools—others who follow
   B. Julie Boergers—co-director—Pediatric Sleep Program—Hasbro Children's Hospital
      1. Later start—decrease—depression—car accidents—dropouts—lateness—absences—improve academics and well-being!
   C. 201 higher schoolers—research—30 minutes later
      1. Students who got 8 hours: performance rose—39%—lateness dropped—50%—sleepiness dropped—29%—incredible! ***(PAUSE)***
   D. Additional sleep—strive—academically
      1. New England—3,000—students—slept more—better grades
         a. 17–33 minutes more per night—"Bs"
         b. Lower grades—2.3 hours later—compared with "A/B" students—remarkable!

PAUSE! FINISH STRONG! YOU CAN DO THIS!

Conclusion

IV. In conclusion,
   A. Early start time—negative effects
   B. How we can implement this change in policy?
   C. Benefits of later start time
V. With your help and others who fight for the betterment of students and their health, we can change this policy for the better!
VI. THANK YOU!

Research Notes

"Sleep and Teens." *UCLA Sleep Disorders Center, UCLA Health.* **www.uclahealth.org/sleepcenter/sleep-and-teens.**

- Sleep deprivation
  - Teens do not get the sleep that they need
  - Teens—important phase of their growth and development
  - "The average teen needs about 9 hours of sleep each night to feel alert and well rested."
- Circadian rhythms
  - Occurs in a 24-hour cycle
  - Makes you feel sleepy/alert
  - Internal clock tells your body when it is time to sleep at night and wake up in the morning
    - Teens affect their internal clocks
      - Staying up late
      - Changes in schedules of falling asleep and waking up
        - Become sleep when they should be awake
        - Fall asleep at school, work, or when driving
- Puberty
  - Body changes
  - Average age is 10–11
    - Boys
      - Typically delayed after females
    - Girls
      - Signs of puberty as early as 7–8 years old
  - Affects circadian rhythm
    - Before puberty
      - Body makes you tired around 8:00/9:00 p.m.
    - Puberty begins
      - Rhythm shifts later; body makes you tired around 10:00/11:00 p.m.
- Normal activities that teens do that impact sleep
  - Early class times for schools
  - Hours of homework after school
  - Work after school
  - Sports, clubs, and activities
  - Time with friends
  - Staying out too late, drinking, smoking
- Struggles with early time/tiredness
  - Wake up and be on time for school
  - "The need for an alarm clock to wake up is a sign that they are not getting enough sleep at night."
  - Fall asleep during class

Ritcher, Ruthann. "Among Teens, Sleep Deprivation an Epidemic." *Stanford Medicine News Center*, **October 8, 2015. med.stanford.edu/news/all-news/2015/10/among-teens-sleep-deprivation-an-epidemic.html.**

- Example
  - Stays up to midnight completing homework
  - Struggles to stay awake during class and focusing on what he or she is learning
  - "You feel tired and exhausted, but you think you just need to get through the day so you can go home and sleep"
  - Cycle
    - After school = catching up on work, plus homework, and then not getting enough sleep
- 2006 National Sleep Foundation poll
  - 87% of high school students get less sleep than 8–10 hours
    - Affects health, safety, and academics.
    - Sleep deprivation
      - Depression, poor grades, accidents, hard to concentrate, anxiety, thoughts of suicide
- William Dement, MD, PhD, founder of Stanford Sleep Disorders Clinic
  - "It is a huge problem. What it means is that nobody performs at the level they could perform, whether it is in school, on the roadways, on the sports field, or in terms of physical and emotional health."
- "According to a 2011 sleep poll, by the time students reach 12th grade, they are sleeping an average of 6.9 hours a night, down from an average of 8.4 hours in the sixth grade."
- Sleep deprivation
  - Increase in impulsive behavior due to a lack of development of the frontal lobe.
- University of Minnesota study in 1990
  - High school start times from 7:20 a.m. to 8:30 a.m.
  - Results
    - Students felt less depressed, sleepy, and motivated
    - Increase in attendance rates, and students got 5 more hours of sleep each week.
- American Academy of Pediatrics—2014
  - Encouraged middle and high schools to start no earlier than 8:30 a.m. to "help preserve the nation's youth."
- Suicide
  - Sleep problems can cause suicidal thoughts and death by suicide
  - 3rd cause of fatalities among 15–24-year-olds
  - Rebecca Bernert, PhD, directs the Suicide Prevention Research Lab at Stanford
    - "Sleep may affect the way in which teens process emotions"
    - Her work shows that lack of sleep can make people more responsive to negative emotional information.

"CDC: Most Middle and High School Students Don't Get Enough Sleep." *American Physical Therapy Association*, January 29, 2018, www.apta.org/PTinMotion/News/2018/01/29/CDCSleep/.

- CDC
  - Middle school children
    - Lack of sleep can increase the risk of health problems such as obesity, diabetes, and injury.
- Youth Risk Behavior Surveys (YRBS)—2015
  - Surveyed middle and high schools' students in 39 states about how many hours of sleep they got on a school night
    - Results
      - Middle school students
        - 57.8%—lack of sleep
        - 12%—fewer than 6 hours a night
      - High school students
        - 72.7%—lack of sleep
        - 20%—fewer than 6 hours a night
- Delayed school start times
  - Recommended by the American Academy of Pediatrics, the American Medical Association, and the American Academy of Sleep Medicine

Rabinowitz, Phil. "Section 9. Changing Policies in Schools." *Chapter 25. Changing Policies | Section 9. Changing Policies in Schools | Main Section | Community Toolbox*. ctb.ku.edu/en/table-of-contents/implement/changing-policies/school-policies/main.

- School system/schools—hierarchical
  - School Committee
    - Decide system-wide policies
  - Superintendent of Schools
    - Carries out policies
  - Assistant Superintendents
  - Other system-wide administrators (coordinators of curriculum, athletics, special education, business, physical plant)
  - Principals
    - Decide policies just for their school
  - Teachers and other professional employees (nurses, guidance counselors and school psychologists, coaches)
  - Support and custodial staff
- Why change policies in schools?
  - To improve student's physical/mental health, sleep, education, classroom, and school climate
- When should you advocate for change?
  - Before the beginning of a new school year
- Who should be involved in changing school policies?
  - Students, parents, the school committee, the superintendent, other school administrators, teachers, groups interested in the change (doctors, medical researchers), and citizens

- How do you change policies in schools?
  - Gather people who support your proposal
  - Strategize
    - Gather ideas and plans through communication
  - Learn about the current policy thoroughly
    - Research the logistics of the policy on start times
  - Learn about the school system, how it works, and the people involved
    - Research how decisions are made within the system, so you know who to target and persuade the most
  - What policy will you replace it with?
    - Starting schools later
    - Explain the benefits, why this change is necessary, how benefits outweigh the cost, and show the importance of this change.
  - Draft the policy you want
    - Specifically show what you want in a later start time
  - Start persuading people at the lowest level of the hierarchy
  - Present the policy change at a school committee meeting
    - Gain support via media from supporters
    - Be prepared for opposing arguments
  - The school committee has to approve and institute the change

Nicosia, Mareesa. "A Start School Later Success Story in Missouri: Higher Graduation Rates, Fewer Suspensions." *The 74 A Start School Later Success Story in Missouri Higher Graduation Rates Fewer Suspensions Comments*, January 6, 2016, www.the74million.org/article/a-start-school-later-success-story-in-missouri-higher-graduation-rates-fewer-suspensions/.

- Example
  - Jilly Dos Santos—sophomore in high school in Missouri
    - "I had trouble waking up in the morning and trouble getting to bed at night, which is a prime example of what early start times can do to adolescents"
  - In 2013, convinced the school board on why starting at 7:20 a.m. is bad
    - Backed up with evidence and many supporters via social media
    - Officials moved the start time to 8:55 a.m. for 4 high schools
    - Created publicity via social media, and an email blast to teachers and friends
  - Results
    - Principal Kim Presko
      - "Our kids seem to be more awake and more eager to learn"
    - Superintendent Peter Stiepleman
      - "The number of annual out-of-school suspensions has dropped by nearly 1,000 and graduation rates rose from 82.7% to 90.2%"

Boergers, Julie. "Benefits of Later School Start Times." *Brown University Child & Adolescent Behavior Letter*, vol. 31, no. 1, Jan. 2015, pp. 1-6. *EBSCOhost*, Holy Family University Library.

- Julie Boergers, PhD—professor in the Departments of Psychiatry and Human Behavior and Pediatrics at the Alpert Medical **School** of Brown University, and co-director of the Pediatric Sleep Program at Hasbro Children's Hospital.
  - Adolescents require about 8.5 to 9.5 hours of sleep
    - According to the National Sleep Foundation, only 14% sleep this amount, and 70% sleep less than 8 hours during the week
  - Sleep deprivation
    - Impacts learning, memory, motivation, and academic performance.
  - Starting school later
    - More sleep
    - Lower rates of depression, car accidents, dropouts, absences, lateness,
    - Improvements in standardized test scores and quality of life
  - Example (her own study)
    - School started at 8:00 a.m. but changed to 8:25 a.m.
    - Results
      - Reduces depressed mood, caffeine use, daytime napping, lateness, and falling asleep during class
      - Students got 29 more minutes of sleep per night
      - Percentage of students receiving 8 hours of sleep doubled
      - Bedtimes did not change
      - Later start had no effect on the amount of time students played sports, activities, and homework
        - Felt less tired and more energized

"Improve Your Child's School Performance with a Good Night's Sleep." *Sleepfoundation.org*, *National Sleep Foundation*, https://www.sleepfoundation.org/children-and-sleep/sleep-and-school-performance.

- Succeed academically
  - Need energy, focus, concentration, retain information, and so on
- Experiment
  - Children were asked to go to bed later than normal and then another week of sleeping for 10 hours
  - For later bedtimes, teachers said they had academic and attention problems
- Study of 1,000 children and preadolescents
  - Measured kids' sleep and school performance
  - Kids who had difficulty going to bed and had been waking up during the night had worse school achievement

- Fatigue = school failure
- Study of 3,000 high school students in New England
  - More sleep = better grades
    - Students with higher grades slept more and went to bed earlier
    - Bs or better
      - 17–33 minutes more sleep and went to bed 10–50 minutes earlier during the week
    - Lower grades/weekends
      - Went to bed on average 2.3 hours later compared to A/B students, who went to bed 1.8 hours later

Tanner, Lindsey. "Study Shows Teens Benefit from Later School Day." *The Call*, July 5, 2010. ProQuest SIRS Issues Researcher, Holy Family University Library.

- 30 extra minutes of sleep
  - More alertness in class, better moods, less lateness, and healthier breakfasts
- Deepest sleep occurs around dawn
  - Students wake up around that time for school; hence, they are groggy
- 201 high schoolers completed surveys before and after change
  - 8:00 a.m. to 8:30 a.m.; classes cut 5 to 10 minutes to avoid longer school
  - Results
    - Students who got 8 hours of sleep during the week rose from 16% to 55%
    - Daytime sleepiness dropped from 49% to 20%
    - Lateness's dropped by 50%
    - Students felt less depressed and irritated

"Success Stories." *Start School Later*, Start School Later Inc., 2020. www.startschoollater.net/success-stories.html.

- Schools in 46 states changed their start time to later
- Suggests time to be after 8:30 a.m.
- Range from the years 2011–2018
- Majority of times were moved to 8:30 a.m.
  - Some 8:00 a.m.
- Example in PA
  - Mechanicsburg
    - High school
      - 8:20 a.m.–3:20 p.m. instead of 7:55 a.m.–2:57 p.m.
    - Middle school
      - 8:30 a.m.–3:30 p.m. instead of 8:20 a.m.–3:20 p.m.

Outline Template

Title

Introduction

    I. Hook with topic reveal
   II. Connect topic to yourself
  III. Connect topic to your audience
  IV. *For Persuasive Speeches Only:* Include Questionnaire findings and address target audience
   V. Thesis

Body

    I. Main Point
      A. Fill in and reorganize sub-points and
         1. Sub-sub-points as you develop each main point.
      B. Remember that every speech will have a different number of main points.
      C. Each main point will also have a different number of corresponding sub- and sub-sub-points.
         1. Consider the "template" for the body of your speech to necessarily need to adjust to fit the content of your writing!
   II. Main Point (with sub- and sub-sub-points)
  III. Main Point (with sub- and sub-sub-points)
  IV. Main Point (with sub- and sub-sub-points)

Conclusion

    I. In conclusion,
      A. Review main points you covered in your speech
   II. Remind us why we should care about what we just learned
  III. Sendoff
  IV. Thank you!

Research Notes

A list of MLA Format citations of all the sources you consulted in your research for this speech, spaced and indented like this entry, and using Purdue OWL to follow the most up-to-date MLA Guidelines.

- Each citation should be followed by a bullet-pointed list of the notes you took and quotations you encountered and planned to include while researching for the speech.

- The reason to keep research notes organized by source as you work on your speech is two-fold:
  - It ensures that you do not forget which sources taught you which pieces of information.
  - You will keep these notes as you work on your research, helping you to "see what you plan to say" as you work. In short, keeping notes organized by source helps you with generating and organizing your main points.
- Each speech will have a different number of required resources. Consult Canvas Assignment details to ensure you do not lose points for not conducting your research thoroughly and according to the Assignment parameters.

Conclusion with Sample Exercises

Now that you know how to generate your main points, what your instructor expects of your speech outline, and how to organize your research notes, it is time for you to start drafting your own speech outline! Remember to use the **outline template** provided above; remember to start by keeping active **research notes** as you gather information and build your main points. The final step is to generate your **thesis**, which **previews** the **main points** you will cover in the speech, while also stating their importance and relevance. And always remember to check your instructor's assignment descriptions to make sure you are completing assignments completely and correctly.

Still want more practice outlining before you jump in and begin working on your own? Here are some sample exercises to help strengthen your outlining skills:

1. Watch Rihanna's acceptance speech for the 2020 NAACP Image Awards (https://www.youtube.com/watch?v=fZiyZ2rDdv8). Then reorganize this outline (which is currently out of order, and which does not include delivery cues) so that the outline reflects the structure of Rihanna's original speech.

III. Can't let de-sensitivity seep in; the idea that "If it's not your problem, then it is not mine."
b. How many of us…partners, colleagues…other races, sexes, religions…show of hands.
a. Bigger than just me, but not than us.
i. Can only fix world together, not divided.
II. Tonight is not really about me.
V. Thank you to NAACP for your efforts to ensure equality for our communities. Thank you for celebrating our strength and tenacity. We have been denied opportunities since the beginning of time, and still we prevail. Imagine what we could do together.
a. Women's problem, black people's problem, poor people problem.
I. Thank you, Derrick and to the community and staff board of the NAACP, including all of you guys here in this room and everyone at home watching who has devoted their lives and efforts toward supporting people of color.
i. This is your problem, too.
IV. When we are marching and protesting and posting about Michael Brown Jr. and Atatiana Jefferson, tell your friends to "pull up."
b. My part: Clara Lionel Foundation in 2012.

2. Using the **outline template** above, watch "Medical Robots" (https://www.youtube.com/watch?v=nPgQsMdWg_8) and create an outline for that informative speech.

Your task is to pretend that you are the student who wrote this speech. So try not to do things like analyze pathos or otherwise comment on delivery. Rather, fill in each part of the outline with the content you hear presented.

Don't worry about filling in the research notes. Do try to think about what delivery cues this speaker may have left themselves on their notecards. Follow your Informative Outline Draft assignment guidelines in terms of what to write as full sentences and what to write as phrases:

- Please write the following in full sentences:
    - Hook
    - Thesis
        - In an Informative Speech, your thesis will involve concisely previewing your main points, while also making clear why you believe your topic is important.
    - Main Points/Connectives
    - Oral Citations/Quotations/Statistics
    - Sendoff
- No need to write the following in full sentences
    - Sub-points
    - Sub-sub-points
    - Summary of main points in conclusion

Chapter 4
Writing for Science and Labs

Overview of Chapter:

I. Introduction to Science Writing
II. Types of Scientific Writing
   A. Writing a Testable/Falsifiable Hypothesis
   B. Independent and Dependent Variables
   C. Types of Data Visualization
   D. Formatting Figures
   E. Labels and Captions
   F. Formatting Tables
III. Review 1—Grammar and Writing Style
   G. Writing Style and Voice
   H. Jargon
   I. Quotes
   J. Identifying and Avoiding Plagiarism
   K. Scientific Nomenclature
   L. Section Autonomy
IV. Review 2—Formatting Checklist

Introduction to Science Writing

Science is an approach to understanding natural phenomena. It is a way of knowing about the world through testing hypotheses. Since performing science requires a particular approach, the **scientific method**, science writing requires a particular approach as well. Knowing how to create clear, descriptive, and direct scientific writing is important. The data collected during the experiment and used to create figures are only half of the process. The next part of the process is the actual writing. Scientific writing puts your data into a larger scientific context, describes the results, and provides explanations of the significance. The results of the study can have important implications for society, public health, and the environment, but you have to be able to convey your message clearly, effectively, and accurately.

Science is a systematic way to study how things work. The scientific method begins with an observation or a question followed by a hypothesis, experimentation, and conclusion. The conclusion supports or does not support the original question. Either way, this leads to more questions and observations. Followed by an additional hypothesis and more experiments.

Yes, it is a never-ending loop, because in the scientific world, there are always unanswered questions. If the universe is expanding faster than the speed of light (Whiting 2004) or if the strings in string theory were blown to the size of a person, the size of a proton would be the entire galaxy (Becker et al. 2007), you can imagine there is a lot of science in between that needs to be filled, and biologist and biochemists are only working on a tiny fraction of the entire scale.

Types of Scientific Writing

Surprisingly, there are many forms of scientific writing. People even have careers as scientific writers. Scientists write everything from peer-reviewed journal articles to grant proposals and literature reviews. You may be asked to draw upon some of them as you are writing. Writing a lab report for your courses is one of the simplest forms of scientific writing and is an important part of learning how to communicate science. The main goal is to truthfully report what has been performed in the laboratory and draw a conclusion based on your observations and findings. The body of a lab report has six major sections which appear as follows: Abstract, Introduction, Methods, Results, Discussion, and Conclusion. In this chapter, we will guide you through the step-by-step process of writing your lab report.

> **STEP 1.** (In Lab) Review the background Information, identify the **Research Question,** and formulate a **Hypothesis**

Writing a Testable/Falsifiable Hypothesis

In your classroom laboratory, your instructor likely has given you a protocol describing the procedure you will be using. In addition to the procedure, the lab protocol usually provides background information on the scientific principle the lab is designed to demonstrate. A laboratory report is based on research around a testable and falsifiable hypothesis. This background information should be used to formulate a hypothesis before you begin your experimentation. A hypothesis is a testable and falsifiable statement that explains some observed phenomenon in nature (Strode 2015). A testable hypothesis should be based on some initial observations. For example, let us think out a simple experiment; when you threw an apple, it fell down to the ground. You realized no matter where you threw the apple, it always fell down. Then you started testing other objects around the house—pillows, socks, jackets, toys—and invariably, everything fell down. At this moment, you observed a pattern, and you came up with the hypothesis—household objects fell down. The initial observations for a lab report may be based on background research that you have done or the background information that your instructor provided to you.

What makes this hypothesis testable? Well for most of the household objects, you can pick it up and drop it and observe where it goes. That is your test. You may have a hunch that the refrigerator or the washing machine will behave similarly, but without help with a strong person or a forklift, it is nearly impossible to lift those appliances and do your experiment (please do not do these experiments because those are expensive to replace). Therefore, your next hypothesis, which could include the heavier appliances in the household—that they will also fall if dropped—becomes non-testable given the current experimental condition. Such constraints exist widely and range from why we cannot test viruses such as SARS-cov-2 on campus due to the lack of Level-4 biosafety lab, to why the string theory remains just a theory (Foster 2020).

To provide another example, let's say you are examining how seagrass density affects predation in clam populations. You could formulate the following *testable* hypothesis:

> *I hypothesize that if denser habitat provides refuge for prey, predation on clams will be lower in dense seagrass.*
> It can be helpful to phrase your hypothesis in a "If…then" manner. If *a particular scientific principle* is happening, then *the following prediction* will occur.

You can test this hypothesis by manipulating the seagrass density and measuring predation. A hypothesis that isn't testable, may be vague, or may not include any variables to manipulate can be described with the following example:
Clam predation could be lower.

There are two issues in this hypothesis. The word "could" makes it a vague non-definitive statement. In addition, the use of the word "lower" without another variable makes the hypothesis not testable as written. What is meant by lower? Lower than what? Lower than last year? Lower than mussels? There is no way to test this hypothesis as it is written.

As we noted, the second criteria for a good hypothesis is that it is *falsifiable*. A falsifiable hypothesis is one that can be refuted. In other words, the data collected from your experiment may show your hypothesis to be false. Returning to our clam example, if we find predation on clams to be higher in less dense seagrass, then our hypothesis is false and therefore the data would refute the hypothesis. If there is nothing that *could* happen to refute your hypothesis, it is not falsifiable and therefore does not meet the criteria of a good hypothesis.

Another common mistake that students sometimes make when writing hypotheses is to list every possible outcome so that they are not *wrong* about the results of the experiment. So long as a hypothesis is relevant, testable, and falsifiable it cannot be wrong in the traditional sense. If your results refute your hypothesis that is totally OK! It is not wrong; it is just not supported by your data. It will give you something to write about later in the conclusion. In our example, your hypothesis would be supported if you find that clam predation is lower in less dense seagrass and higher in more dense seagrass. Your hypothesis would be refuted if you find the opposite in your experiment. It is worth noting that here we wrote our hypothesis in the first person and very clearly communicated that this was our hypothesis by starting the sentence with the phrase "I hypothesize…." The hypothesis should not be a secret, and it's important for the reader to identify the hypothesis easily so it's best to be blunt here.

> STEP 2. Write the Methods section of your lab report

The purpose of a lab report is to communicate the findings of your research clearly so they can be replicated by other scientists. Therefore, the methods section is one of the most important sections in your report. A good writing tip for the methods section is to write it first even though it does not appear first. It is also wise to write your methods as soon as you can after the experiment has been performed so the experiment is fresh in your memory. The methods section should be written with paragraph structure, using a narrative style. Avoid using bulleted lists or number lists that you may find in the protocol from your class. You'll want to transform your protocol into a readable description of what you did, including the equipment used in your experiment. Here again, do not use a number or bulleted list to communicate your equipment or materials. Simply talk about the materials used as you describe how you performed the experiment. For example,

> *[Ten clams were added to each plot. Clams were between 8 and 12 mm, the preferred size for juvenile blue crabs (Arnold 1984), and marked with a small dab of white paint to facilitate recapture. Control treatments were covered with plastic 0.65 cm mesh to exclude predators.]* (Rielly-Carroll and Freestone 2017)

In the experiment described above the materials (clams, paint, and plastic mesh) are described as they are used in the experiment, not in a separate list.

The methods section provides the information needed so that someone could repeat your experiment. If your methods are not clear or not accurate, it is very likely other researchers may find your result irreproducible, and the cost may not just be your reputation but also a great waste to the society in general (Freedman et al. 2015). A good and precise piece of writing in the methods section should cover the details of all reagents, including the origin of each reagent, the make and model of any instrument that is used, the time length and temperature of each experiment, and so on. There are never more details; the more the merrier. If you performed any statistical analyses or calculations, you'll also want to include that information in the methods. Just as a reminder, make sure you stay away from describing any results. In the methods section, you describe what you did but not the data you produced.

> STEP 3. Analyze your data and write your results section

The results section of your laboratory report is the most objective section, and it should be free of any interpretation. For this reason, besides tables and figures that you may include, the results section may be the shortest of your report. Simply state the results of your experiment as they are, refrain from stating whether the results were interesting, surprising, and support or refute your hypothesis.

Independent versus Dependent variables

In an experiment there are usually two main variables being addressed: independent variable and dependent variable. The independent variable is the one that you are manipulating or changing. The dependent variable is the one that you are measuring in response to the change in the independent variable.

> **Hypothesis**
>
> *I hypothesize that if denser habitat provides refuge for prey, predation on clams will be lower in dense seagrass.*

Using our clam-seagrass example, the independent variable is the seagrass density—this is the one that is manipulated or changed. The dependent variable is predation on clams—this is the one that we are measuring in response to the change in seagrass. As you are writing and building your tables or graphs make sure that you know which variable is the dependent and which variable is the independent.

Types of Data Visualizations

Long articles can be boring to read. When you start reading a magazine journal, what is the first thing that catches your eye? Pictures? So, the adage, "A picture is worth a thousand words," holds true for scientific writing as well. The pictures in your article are meant to support the scientific argument you are making. Pictures in scientific writing can include data represented in a graph, images of focal organisms, maps of sampling sites, or a schematic or diagram of a proposed model. These images will help convey your overall message and help the reader understand the purpose of your writing.

You will first determine the best type of graph to represent your data. The visual representation of your data is important to make sure the results are clear to the reader. There are many types of graphs, and determining the best option will allow your data to be understood. If you are tracking changes over time, a good option would be the bar graph or line graph. A bar graph will be helpful if your changes are large, and smaller changes are better-tracked on a line graph. A stacked bar graph is more appropriate if you are comparing a part to the whole. It is important to choose the correct type of graph so your data are represented correctly and clearly. Although the three most commonly used graphs include the line graph, bar graph, and scatter plots, there are several options laid out in Table 1. It is important to choose the best graph to avoid the reader misinterpreting your data.

TABLE 1 Commonly used graphs in scientific writing.

Type of Graph	Best Use
Line Graph	To show small trends between variables. To make predictions over time. Comparing two or more variables.
Bar Graph	To show large differences between groups. One variable is a category.
X-Y Scatter Plot	To determine if there is a relationship between two variables.
Stacked Bar Graph	Represent composition of something.

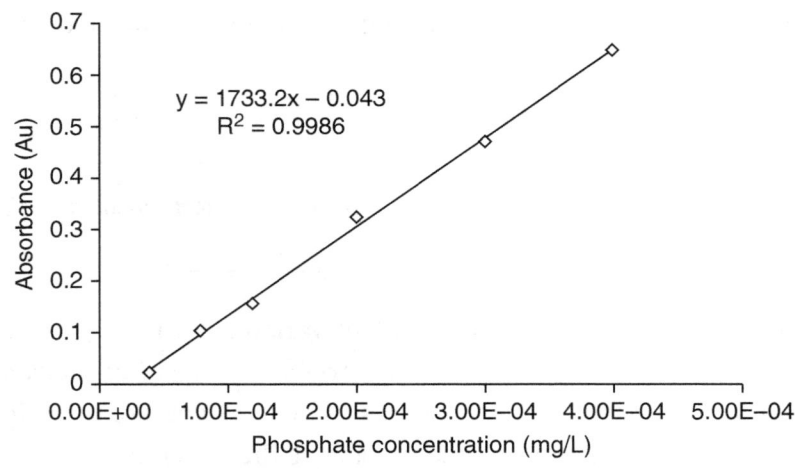

FIGURE 1 Standard curve for phosphate. Absorbance increases as phosphate concentration increases

For ease, we will discuss the steps to create a line graph or bar graph. These graphs can be easily prepared using either Microsoft Excel or Google Sheets. Let's first look at the steps to create a **line graph.** A line graph is best used in situations that show a relationship between two variables or need to monitor the trend against a variable, such as time or concentration. For example, when measuring the concentration of a certain chromophoric compound (a compound that either has color or interacts with ultraviolet light) in the chemistry lab we use a spectrophotometer. Solutions of various concentrations are prepared and then the corresponding absorbance is measured. To clearly show the data, we can come up with a linear graph as the shown in the following example (conveniently referred to as a calibration curve). In Figure 1, the concentration of the chromophoric compound (phosphate) is plotted on the X-axis and the absorbance is plotted on the Y-axis. The graph shows a clear linear relationship between the phosphate concentration and the absorbance. As the concentration increases so does the absorbance.

In this graph, concentration is the independent variable, and absorbance is the observed term against the variable or dependent variable. This graph clearly shows the trend that with increasing concentration, the absorbance also increases.

A second type of graph is the **bar graph.** A bar graph is in many ways similar to the line graph, as it allows you to compare two variables. Bar graphs are better when differences in your data are larger (line graphs will help to show smaller changes). Bar graphs can also be useful when one of your variables is a category, rather than numeric. For example, in Figure 2, we see the average clam mortality in low- and high-density seagrass. Seagrass density in this example is a categorical variable. Similarly to the line graph, the independent variable (seagrass density) is plotted on the X-axis and the dependent variable (clam mortality) is plotted on the Y-axis.

Formatting Figures

In scientific writing, both images and data visualizations of any type are considered "figures" (tables are not included in this designation). Figures should be numbered sequentially (i.e., 1, 2, 3 …) in the order that they are discussed in your text. All figures included in your lab report should be referenced in the text. If you don't write about it in the lab report, it shouldn't be in it. There are two

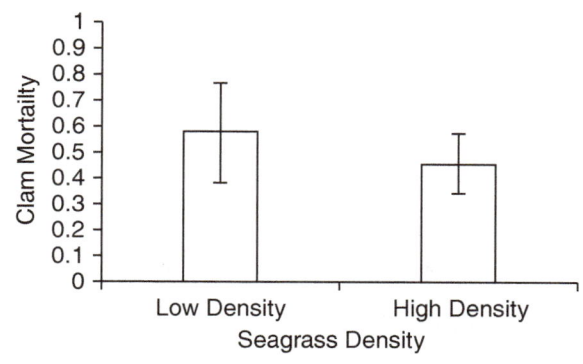

FIGURE 2 Clam mortality is higher in low-density seagrass ($n = 10$)

ways that you can reference a figure in your writing, as the subject of your sentence or parenthetically. For example,

As the subject:
Figure 2 shows predation on clams is higher in less dense seagrass.
Parenthetically:
Predation on clams is higher in less dense seagrass (Fig. 2).

Labels and Captions

When you insert a figure it should be labeled with a figure number and caption directly below the figure. An easy way to do this in Microsoft Word is to first insert a "text box" and then paste your figure inside the textbox and write the caption below the figure. This will keep your figure and caption together as you format your document. In google docs, you can insert a "drawing." When you are in the drawing space you can paste your figure and write a caption. The two items are then saved together. Formatting images, such as Figure 3, follows the same guidelines as graphs. If the image is not your own, provide a source in the caption.

FIGURE 3 Adult hard clams (*Mercenaria mercenaria*) range in size from 3 to 5 inches (NOAA.gov)

TABLE 2 Components in the atmosphere

Components in atmosphere	Percentage
Nitrogen	78.084
Oxygen	20.946
Argon	0.934
carbon dioxide	0.041332
Neon	0.001818
Helium	0.000524
Methane	0.000187
Krypton	0.000114

A. Tables

Tables are also important for organizing data. In general, if the data set can be presented against a single variable, a graph is much easier to read than the data table. This is not to say that data tables are unimportant; on the contrary, data tables may contain important nuances that are often overlooked in the graphs.

Table 2 shows the makeup of gases in the atmosphere. As a matter of fact, these greenhouse gases (Doll 2011) are very important to climate change that affects our daily lives and must be considered; another figure, such as a pie graph, simply would not do the trick because it may not adequately show very small numbers. Below is an example of a table that shows the composition of a few more gases in the atmosphere (Haynes 2016):

Formatting Tables

In scientific writing, including lab reports, tables have a very specific format so that they are readable and consistent. Like figures, tables should be numbered consecutively (i.e., Table 1, 2, 3 …) in the order that they are discussed in the text of your report. Only tables that are discussed in the text of your report should be included. Again, like figures, tables should be referenced in the text either as the subject of your sentence or parenthetically. Tables should have a clear, informative title that follows the table number. Tables differ from figures in that this information goes *above* the table. As you may have noticed in Table 1, the borders of a scientific table have a specific format style. Tables should only utilize a few horizontal lines as borders. There are no vertical lines in the tables at all. Typically a table will have a top and bottom border, and a border underneath the variables, separating the variables from the data.

STEP 4. Develop an Introduction

The introduction will guide the reader into the research topic and provides necessary information to understand the current study. The introduction should communicate to the reader where your study fits into the larger scientific community. What do we already know about the topic at hand?

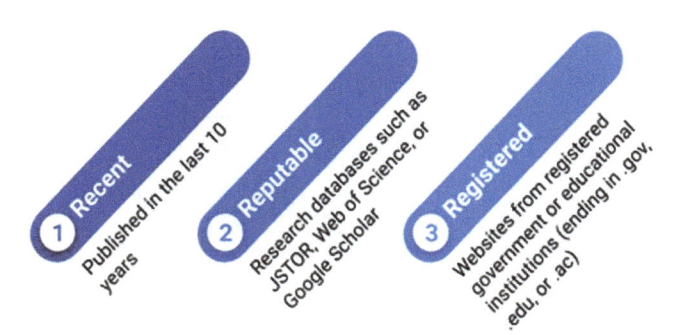

FIGURE 4 The three Rs of credible sources

1. Recent — Published in the last 10 years
2. Reputable — Research databases such as JSTOR, Web of Science, or Google Scholar
3. Registered — Websites from registered government or educational institutions (ending in .gov, .edu, or .ac)

What is the main scientific theory or principle being explored in the lab exercise? Why is this new study important? A good introduction should include a short survey of the current field. The reader should feel familiar with the topic and have all necessary information required to understand your research question and hypothesis.

Before you begin the actual writing for the introduction, the first step is to collect background information. It can be helpful to think about writing a lab report as if you are answering an unknown question. As writers, we want to point out to the reader in a clear way why the question is important to answer. To do so, we must use existing research to provide relevant background information and significance. Science writing is known for being simple and concise, and for a scientist, the most important things to include are verifiable facts. It is important to make sure that the source of the information is credible. So how do we determine if the source information is credible? We can use the three Rs to determine whether or not a particular source is considered credible in the sciences: Recent, Reputable, Registered (Figure 4; Research and Evidence... [date unknown]).

You'll notice this list excludes some common sources such as news articles and websites ending in .com or .org. This doesn't mean you can't use these sources to get started on understanding your topic, but when completing your writing you'll want to rely on credible sources.

Sometimes, your professor may ask you to use *peer-reviewed* literature. Peer-review is an important process in science. Sometimes, it is also called a "refereed" publication. When a scientist submits a paper to a refereed scientific journal, the article begins the peer-review process. Usually, the editor of the journal will send the submission to three other scientists who are experts in the same field. Those scientists will read and comment on the submitted paper. They will decide whether the paper is acceptable, needs revision, or should not be published. The reviewers remain anonymous to the author of the paper, but the author must then incorporate their feedback. Peer-review improves the quality of published science, ensures that the methodology is scientifically sound, and that the results are properly interpreted before publication. One way to easily identify peer-reviewed articles is to use your library's journal database (Holy Family University Library 2020). Usually in the search options you can filter for peer-reviewed articles or journals. Figure 5 shows how to identify the right types of sources for your study.

All statements of fact require support. Providing sources lends credibility to your writing. Use in-text citations throughout your paper to note supporting sources. At the end of your paper, in the references section, you should provide a complete list of all the sources you used in your paper. There are many citation style guides, and they vary across disciplines. A straightforward citation

46 CROSSING DISCIPLINES

Is the source credible?

- Recent / Reputable / Registered
  - Yes → Is it a primary source?
  - No → Don't use it

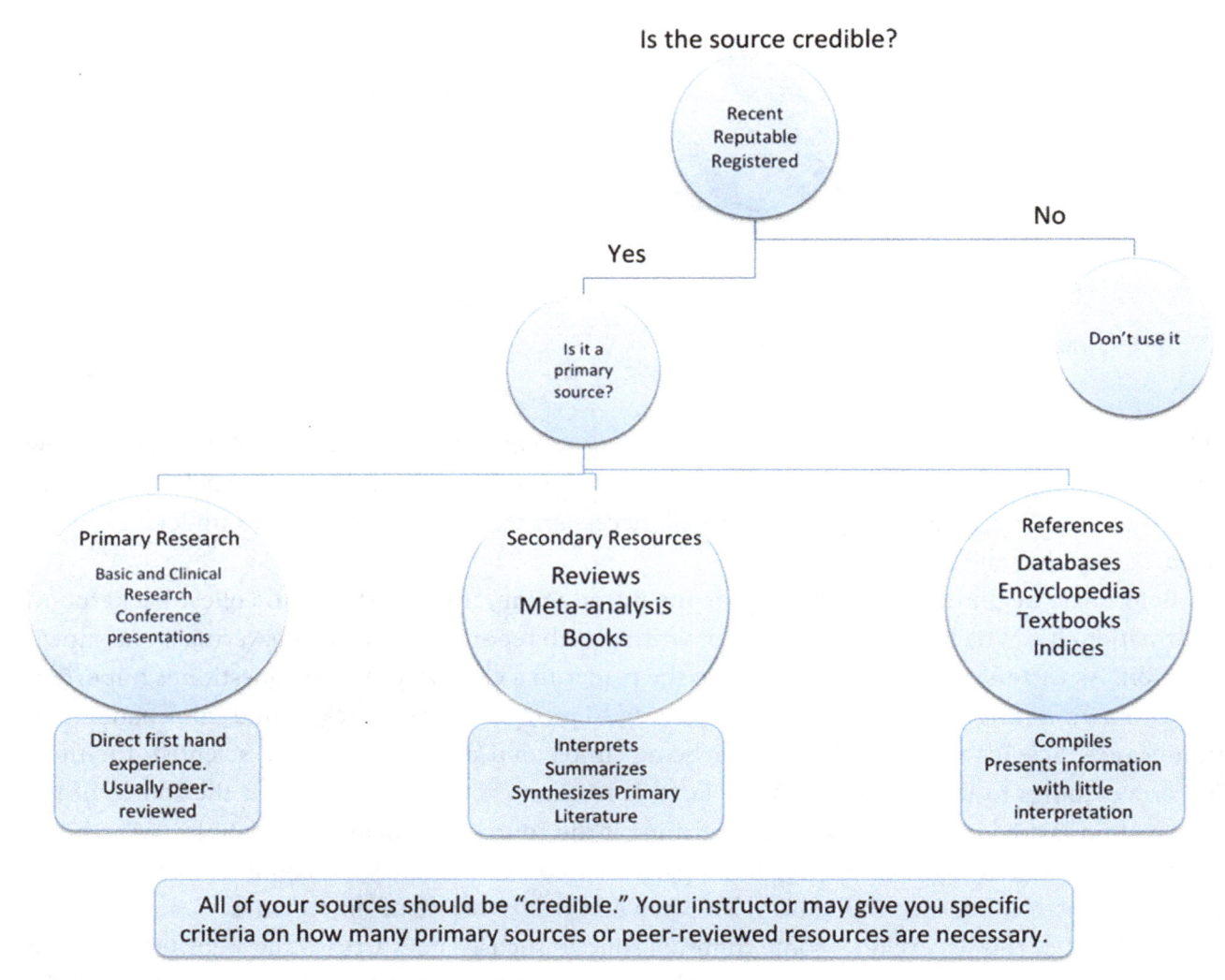

Is it a primary source?

- **Primary Research**: Basic and Clinical Research, Conference presentations — Direct first hand experience. Usually peer-reviewed
- **Secondary Resources**: Reviews, Meta-analysis, Books — Interprets, Summarizes, Synthesizes Primary Literature
- **References**: Databases, Encyclopedias, Textbooks, Indices — Compiles, Presents information with little interpretation

All of your sources should be "credible." Your instructor may give you specific criteria on how many primary sources or peer-reviewed resources are necessary.

FIGURE 5 What resources are right for you? Sources vary in their purpose and perspective

style to use in the sciences is the Council of Science Editors (CSE) Style Guide (2014). In professional science, citation formats required by publishers are often different and very specific to the journal. What's important here is that you cite in-text and provide a complete list of sources using a standard approach.

After you have collected reliable sources, the next step of the introduction is to provide the background information and set the stage for your research question and hypothesis. We can think of the lab report as a whole as having an hourglass shape (Figure 6). The top of the hourglass is the Introduction. The Results and Methods represent the narrowest, most specific part of the hourglass, while the Discussion is the base. When constructing the introduction section of your laboratory report it is good to begin with the broadest topic and work your way to the most specific details related to your research/experiment. All information included in this section will help your reader understand your study better.

The first paragraph should describe the general topic that your lab experiment addressed. Each subsequent paragraph should be more specific. For example, if we did an experiment to determine

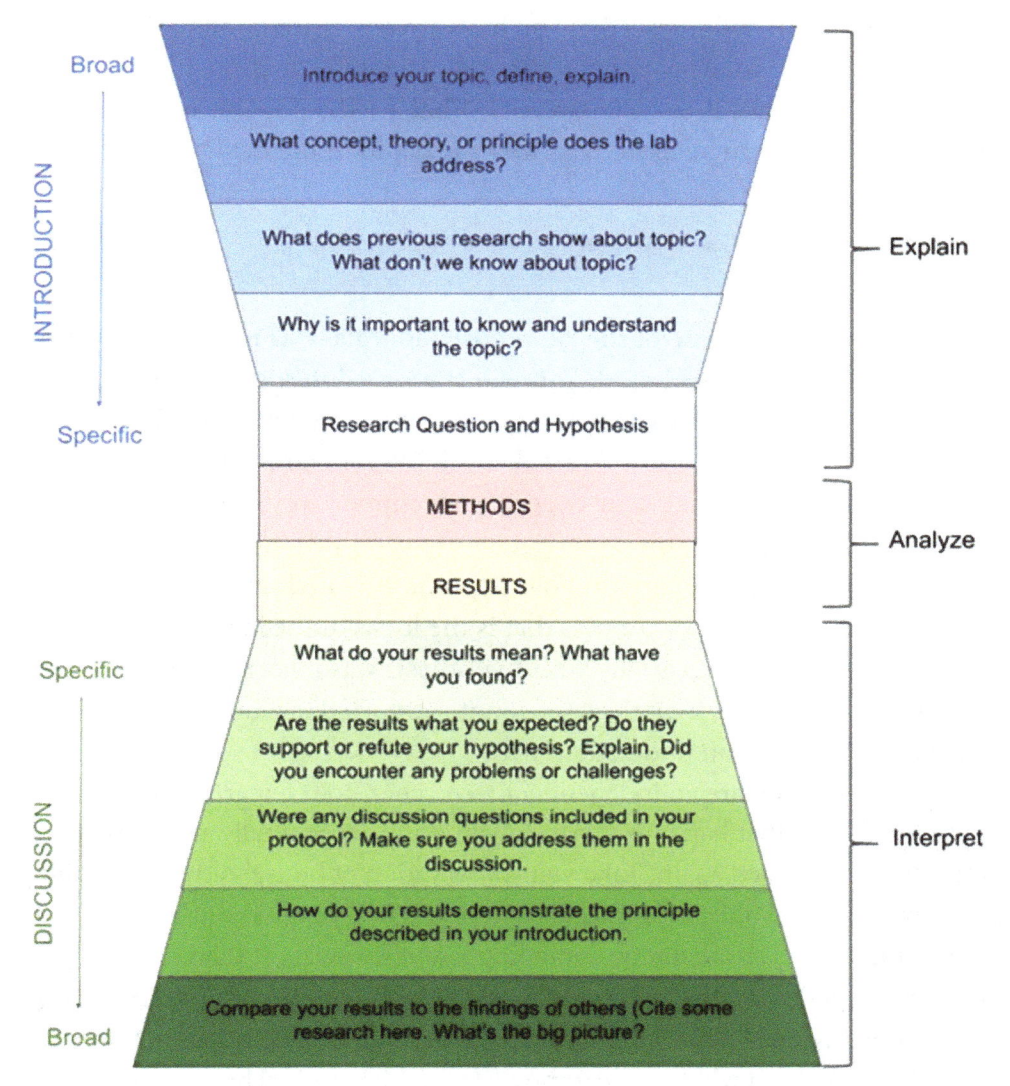

FIGURE 6 Hourglass schematic showing the structure of a scientific lab report

how habitat type affects predation on clams, the first paragraph could be about habitat types, the next on habitat type and predation, and the next on predation and clams, and end with your specific research question about habitat type, predation, and clams. With each paragraph we get more focused until we hone in on our research question. For a lab report, the introduction is your opportunity to demonstrate to your instructor that you understand the concepts from the laboratory. A common mistake that you'll want to avoid in the introduction is to discuss the methods you used or results you produced. The introduction should be free of any description of your experiment or the results.

Another concept that sometimes trips students up is stating that they will "prove" or set out to "prove" a particular phenomenon. When we gather observations or perform experiments in science we are not necessarily proving anything, and that is not the aim of science. We are gathering evidence in order to support or refute the hypothesis we are testing. This may seem like a subtle difference between the words "prove" and "support," but it's an important one that incorporates the nature of the scientific method.

The research question and hypothesis that you have already written follows closely after the introduction. If the introduction is done properly, at the end of the introduction, it becomes almost natural to raise a question, what else needs to be answered? What are the possible blank areas of the current field? What better techniques can be used to further the depth of the field?

STEP 5. Interpret your results and develop your discussion and conclusion

The discussion section is the base of the lab report "hourglass" (Figure 5). As you write this section, you will move from specific to broad. You will start out interpreting your specific results and build a conclusion that addresses how your results fit into or demonstrate the broader scientific principles that the lab was designed to show (Turbek et al. 2016). Here you will interpret your results and draw a conclusion about whether your experiments support your hypothesis or refute it for the first time. In your class laboratories, the experiments are carefully chosen so that you can observe a particular hypothesis. If your results support your hypothesis, you'll want to discuss how your results demonstrate the scientific principle or process that is the focus of the lab. If your data do not support your hypothesis, you'll want to discuss why your hypothesis was incorrect and how the results refute your hypothesis. It is okay if your hypothesis was not supported, as long as you demonstrate in the discussion and conclusion that you understand why.

It's worth noting here, if you are an independent researcher, your experiments may not always agree with your hypothesis. When that happens, what do you do? This generally means that your hypothesis needs to be "modified" and tested again. Take your observation of household objects falling down as an example again; your hypothesis after the initial observation is every household object falls down, and you were able to prove it using experimentation (grabbing it and throwing it then observing where it goes). However, if you were to perform the same experiment in the International Space Station (a very expensive experiment, by the way), you will realize when you release an object, it does not fall any more. At that moment, you should think about what can be improved from the original hypothesis. This is where future work comes in. Should we carry out the same experiment on the moon? Mars? Or Proxima Centauri b? Be aware of the experimentation limitation though, make sure your hypothesis is still testable!

If your instructor provided any discussion questions, you'll want to make sure that you address them in the discussion section in a narrative format (avoid using a question/answer format). As you reach the end of your lab report it is important to state how your results fit into our current scientific knowledge. How do the results of your study compare to the results of other similar studies? Try to zoom out and think of what your results mean in the big picture. What is the broad significance of your work? For example,

Our results demonstrate the importance of habitat structure as a driver of predation intensity, a key biotic interaction.

The intent of the discussion section in the lab report is to demonstrate an understanding of how your experimental outcomes relate to the overarching theme of the lab. It is important to make a direct connection between your data and the scientific concepts at work.

> STEP 6. Write the abstract and title your report

Now that your report is mostly complete, you can write a summary or "abstract." Although the abstract is written last, it appears first in the completed report. The abstract of a paper or laboratory report is the first introduction the reader has to your work. Here you will entice the reader to want to know more. Therefore, the abstract should be informative and descriptive. The abstract is usually a short paragraph, which should include a concise description of the hypothesis, the experimental design, and the major conclusions. There are no surprises in scientific writing. The abstract will tell the brief description of the entire paper and give away the ending. The reader will know exactly if they want to read more to determine the details of the work. The abstract will introduce the reader to the topic, inform about the content, and help readers decide if they want to know more through a short clear summary of the experiment and conclusions. You can see an example of an abstract that follows this format in Figure 7. An abstract is usually less than 250 words, and though it appears first, as we have noted here, we often write this last as it incorporates concepts from each of the lab report sections.

Title

Titles in scientific writing are usually short and concise. The title of your report should tell the reader the hypothesis being tested at a minimum and sometimes even give the results. For example,

The effect of seagrass density on clam predation.

Or

Predation on clams is lower in dense seagrass.

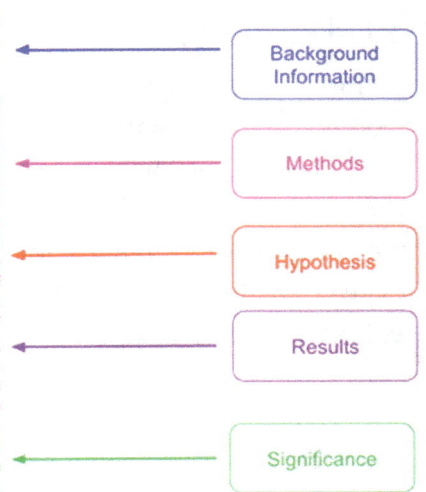

FIGURE 7 Sample annotated abstract (heavily adapted from Nature). Abstract from Rielly-Carroll and Freestone (2017)

STEP 7. Put your completed sections together

Together, the research question, hypothesis, methods, and results represent the narrow part of the hourglass structure of our lab report (Figure 5), meaning these sections are the most specific and narrow in scope and address specifically what you did in the lab—not background information or broad concepts. In your completed report, the order is as follows: Title, Abstract, Introduction, Research Question and Hypothesis, Methods, Results, Discussion, Conclusion (or Summary), and References (list of works that you have cited in the paper's main text, excluding the abstract). There's also, typically, an Acknowledgment section and a Conflict of Interests statement in articles published by research professionals. This may not apply in your case if you are a student and worked on your own for the study and presented the paper only for the perusal of your guides and professors. These two sections appear after the Conclusion and right above the References section. In Acknowledgments author expresses their gratitude for the help received from individuals and organizations to help conduct their study (e.g., universities or federal departments or NGOs and nonprofits that funded their study). In Conflict of Interests, the researcher/author declares that there are NO conflicts of interests, either "professional" or "financial"; that is, the work does not involve any monetary gains for the author or that it will not attract potential loss of any kind (e.g., monetary or otherwise) for the organization/university, in relation to the study conducted.

STEP 8. Proofread and edit your report

It is important to review and edit your lab report once you finish your first draft. You should take the time to review your lab report at least twice. In the first edit, you'll want to read for grammar and style. In the second edit, review formatting and citations.

Review 1—Grammar and Writing Style

G. Writing Style and Voice

The writing style for scientific writing is usually different from fictional writing. Fictional stories are meant to drag you into an imaginary world, where you can free up your creativity and roam freely. Scientific writings, on the other hand, are meant to communicate facts and conclusions based on observations. The key point here is that everything should be factual. Be as concise as possible. Short sentences are the easiest to read. Long sentences can be confusing. In addition, you'll also want to make sure that you've written in a consistent voice. Typically, an active voice is stronger and clearer than a passive voice (ESA). For example,

> Active:
> *We used a mark and recapture predator exposure experiment.*
> Passive:
> *A mark and recapture predator exposure experiment was used.*

The sentence in the active voice is more clear and direct.

Exception, it is also not unusual for journals to demand that Abstract, not the main text, be written in passive voice. Usually, there is always a 'house style guide' provided by the journals for authors to follow prior to submitting their papers for publication, where such exceptions are specified. Your university may have a style guide, too.

H. Jargon

Every discipline has their own jargon, some jargons are just more popular among the general public. For example, practically everyone knows what GDP stands for: Gross Domestic Product. However, not everyone knows the detailed definition of GDP, which is "the total monetary or market value of all the finished goods and services produced within a country's borders in a specific time period" (Chappelow 2020). In the world of science, there are many jargons that are used commonly among biologists and biochemists, and it is assumed that the general public are not familiar with them, except a select few, such as CRISPR (Barragou et al. 2007), a very powerful gene editing tool, although far from perfectly precise so we do not have to worry about X-Men yet.

Every time a jargon is presented in the text, it should be clearly defined and explained to the target audience. For example, for those of you not familiar with CRISPR (and you should ask yourself why), CRISPR stands for Clusters of Regularly Interspaced Short Palindromic Repeats. The whole jargon is somewhat meaningless to most, but if you include the information about the ability for CRISPR-Cas9 to cut based pairs in DNA, you will not need to go very far to get people's attention, because the whole world knows it is bad when a rogue Chinese scientist produced two genetically modified babies using this exact technique (Normile 2019).

I. Quotes

Science writing differs from other disciples in the use of quotes. In other disciplines, sources are often directly cited verbatim through the use of quotations. However, direct quotes are typically not used in science writing. Avoid using direct quotes in science writing. Instead focus on **synthesizing** and **summarizing** the information from your sources and then cite the source.

J. Identifying and Avoiding Plagiarism

Any statement that includes numbers, times, frequencies, or percentages will require a citation for the source of that number.

K. Scientific Nomenclature

You should refer to any organism with its scientific name at least once upon first introduction. Scientific names should **always** be italicized. The first time you name your species you will write the full scientific name. After that you may abbreviate the genus.

Ex. First time—*Ornithorhynchus anatinus*
Second time and forward—*O. anatinus*

L. Section Autonomy

When you are reading through the report, check to make sure each sentence fits appropriately into the section you have written it. Keep your introduction free from results and methods, your methods free from results, and keep the results free from interpretation.

Review 2—Formatting Checklist

- ❑ Graphs and Figures
    - ❑ Captions and figure numbers below the figure
    - ❑ Referenced in the text
    - ❑ Numbered and arranged in the order they are discussed
    - ❑ Both axes are labeled with an axis title and units
    - ❑ No background lines or grids
    - ❑ Legend provided if necessary
- ❑ Tables
    - ❑ Appropriate borders (minimal, horizontal lines dividing titles from data)
    - ❑ Title and number on top of the table
    - ❑ Referenced in the text
    - ❑ Numbered and arranged in the order they are discussed
- ❑ Citations
    - ❑ All facts are followed with a citation
    - ❑ All citations in the text appear in the references list
    - ❑ All citations in the references list appear somewhere in the text
    - ❑ CSE style is properly followed
    - ❑ All references meet the criteria for a "credible" resource
- ❑ Numbers
    - ❑ All measurements have units
    - ❑ Decimals are proceeded with a "0," that is, "0.5 m"
- ❑ Organisms' scientific names are given, and in italics
- ❑ Common abbreviations are named in full upon first appearance, and abbreviated thereafter, that is, Environmental Protection Agency (EPA).

Writing Tips and Resources: http://blogs.nature.com/naturejobs/2016/10/28/scientific-writing-a-very-short-cheat-sheet/

Communicating results with graphs and tables: http://www.clips.edu.au/displaying-data/
http://holyfamily.libguides.com/c.php?g=610229&p=7158199
https://esajournals.onlinelibrary.wiley.com/doi/full/10.1002/bes2.1258#bes21258-bib-0004

References

Barragou, R., Fremaux, C., Deveau, H., Richards, M., Boyaval, P., Moineau, S., Romero, D.A., Horvath, P. CRISPR Provides Acquired Resistance Against Viruses in Prokaryotes. *Science*. 315.5819 (2007): 1709–1712.

Becker, K., Beker, M., Schwarz, J. H. *String Theory and M-Theory: A Modern Introduction*. Cambridge University Press, 2007.

Chappelow, J. Gross Domestic Product—GDP. *Investopedia* [Internet], 2020. https://www.investopedia.com/terms/g/gdp.asp

Council of Science Editors. *Scientific Style and Format: The CSE Manual for Authors, Editors, and Publishers* (8th ed.), 2014.

Doll, J.E., Baranski, M. *Greenhouse Gas Basics, Climate Change and Agriculture Fact Sheet Series*.

Foster, B. Z. *Will String Theory Finally Be Put to the Experimental Test*. Scientific American [Internet], 2020. https://www.scientificamerican.com/article/will-string-theory-finally-be-put-to-the-experimental-test/

Freedman, L.P., Cockburn, I.M., Simcoe, T.S. "The Economics of Reproducibility in Preclinical Research." *Public Library of Science Biology* 13.6 (2015).

Haynes, H.M. ed. *CRC Handbook of Chemistry and Physics* (97th ed.). CRC Press, 2016–2017.

Holy Family University Library. "Peer Reviewed" or "Scholarly" [Internet], 2020. http://holyfamily.libguides.com/c.php?g=610229&p=7158199

Nature. Formatting Guide. *Nature* [Internet], 2020. https://www.nature.com/nature/for-authors/formatting-guide

NOAA. Hard Clam/Northern Quahog, NOAA Fisheries. [Internet], 2020. https://www.fisheries.noaa.gov/species/hard-clam-northern-quahog

Normile, D. "Chinese Scientist Who Produced Genetically Altered Babies Sentenced to 3 Years in Jail." *Science* 2019.

Pechenik, J.A. A Short Guide to Writing About Biology (9th ed.). Pearson-Longman Publishers, 2015.

Purdue University. Using Research and Evidence. *Purdue Online Writing Lab* [Internet], 2020. https://owl.purdue.edu/owl/general_writing/academic_writing/establishing_arguments/research_and_evidence.html

Rielly-Carroll, E., and Freestone, A.L. Habitat fragmentation differentially affects trophic levels and alters behavior in a multi-trophic marine system. *Oecologia* 183.3 (2017): 899–908.

Strode, P. K. "Hypothesis Generation in Biology: A Science Teaching Challenge & Potential Solution." *The American Biology Teacher* 77.7 (2015): 500-506.

Turbek S.P., Chock, T.M., Donahue, K., Havrilla, C.A., Oliverio, A.M., Polutchko, S.K., Shoemaker, L.G., Vimercati, L. Scientific Writing Made Easy: A Step-by-Step Guide to Undergraduate Writing in the Biological Sciences. *The Bulletin of the Ecological Society of America* 97.4 (2016).

Whiting, A.B. "The Expansion of Space: Free Particle Motion and the Cosmological Redshift." *The Observatory* 124 (2004):174.

Chapter 5
APA Formatting in Nursing and Psychology

APA Format 7th Edition

The seventh edition of the APA manual presents two types of papers, both of which are relevant for students. The **professional paper** is to be used when you have conducted an experiment or study and will be writing an introduction, method, results, and discussion section of the paper. This type of paper would be appropriate for courses or circumstances where you are conducting an experiment.

The **student paper** is the type of paper you would write for any other course where you have **not** conducted an experiment, but are writing a research paper. The student paper does not involve collecting data, but rather presenting a thesis and evaluating it throughout your paper. Though both of these papers use a references section, only the professional paper would be appropriate for circumstances where you have collected data and need to evaluate and discuss the implications of the data.

Throughout this chapter, you will see references to the **student paper** and **professional paper** where appropriate.

General APA Formatting

When writing in APA Style, the entire paper should be a 12-point font if you use Times New Roman, if you use Arial then use an 11-point font. The margins should be 1″ all around and the entire paper is double spaced.

APA Style is specific about heading formats as well.

Level	Format
1	**Centered, Bold, Capitalize Each Word** Text begins a new paragraph.
	When You Might Use Level 1 The headings for major sections, like Method, Results, and Discussion.
2	**Flush Left, Bold, Capitalize Each Word** Text begins a new paragraph.
	When You Might Use Level 2 Subheadings within a major section. For example, subheadings in a Method section: Participants, Materials, Procedure.
3	***Flush Left, Bold, Italics, Capitalize Each Word*** Text begins a new paragraph.
	When You Might Use Level 3 If you need to break your subheadings further. For example, you might have level 3 headings within your Materials section, if you have Depression Measures, Anxiety Measures, and Coping Measures.
4	**Indented, Bold, Capitalize Each Word, End With a Period.** Text begins on the same line.
	When You Might Use Level 4. To break the subheadings down further. For example, if you have multiple Depression Measures, you might have level 4 headings for Beck Depression Inventory, Hamilton Depression Inventory, and Center for Epidemiologic Studies Depression Inventory.
5	***Indented, Bold, Italics, Capitalize Each Word, End With a Period.*** Text begins on the same line.
	When You Might Use Level 5. To break down the subheadings one more step. Perhaps for each of your measures, you have multiple Level 5 subheadings to describe each, such as Reliability and Validity, Sample Questions, and Response Options.

©Marta Sher/Shutterstock.com

Title Page (Professional Paper and Student Paper Required)

Professional Title Page

AGE AND GENDER DIFFERENCES
IN ANXIETY   1

Age and Gender Differences in Anxiety

Jennifer DeCicco and Kimberly Dasch-Yee
Holy Family University

Author Note

This work was supported by finding by Holy Family University Grant Number 00012345.

Correspondence should be sent to kdasch-yee@holyfamily.edu

Student Title Page

1

Age and Gender Differences in Anxiety

Jennifer DeCicco
Department of Psychology,
Holy Family University
PSYC 305: Physiological Psychology
Dr. Kimberly Dasch-Yee
October 1, 2020

Abstract (Professional Paper Required; Student Paper Optional)

The abstract is a concise summary of all of the sections of your APA paper. According to APA formatting guidelines in the 7th edition, abstracts should be no more than 250 words. However, it is important to note that each journal and class you take may have different requirements. Please be sure to consult your instructor or the journal submission guidelines. It is important that since it requires information from each section, that you write this section last. That might seem strange, as it is one of the first parts of your paper that is presented. However, until you complete the results and discussion section, you would not know what to write! After writing the other sections of your paper, it would be a good exercise for you to paraphrase each section in roughly two sentences.

Since this is a very short section it is important to convey the most important information.
Here are some important parts that should be highlighted from each section:

Introduction: Summary of major hypotheses; be sure to include the independent and dependent variables.

Method: In one to two sentences summarize who the participants were, the major materials used and how the study was conducted. For example, "Participants included 108 adults between the ages of 18 and 65, who completed an anxiety inventory at multiple time points."

Results: Summarize the results in words without using the statistical information or data.

Discussion: What is the overall implication and impact of this study. Consider mentioning future directions.

Figures/Tables: Are not necessary for the abstract.

The abstract has some basic formatting that differs from the rest of the paper. The abstract always begins on page 2, the word **Abstract** is in bold and centered, and the paragraph is left justified (block format), is double spaced, and usually includes the word *Keywords*: directly under the abstract (tabbed in once). The keywords themselves are in a regular font and in lowercase letters, unless it is a proper noun. The keywords should describe important terms or concepts related to your paper and you should aim to have between three and five keywords total.

Since an abstract is not required for student papers, it would be important to check in with your instructor about specific guidelines or a rubric for the abstract of your paper. When writing an abstract for a student paper, you would approach this in a similar way as a professional paper. However, instead of having space dedicated to the method and results sections, you would focus on the topic/problem/research question, arguments for/against, and concluding remarks.

Introduction (Student Paper and Professional Paper Guidelines)

Your APA Style paper then continues with an Introduction. While it's the second section of the paper as you read it (in a professional paper), it's typically the first section you write. This section explains what's been found before—that's your literature review. The Introduction then ends with a paragraph that briefly explains what you are doing in your own paper.

The first step is the literature review. A literature review is where you describe what researchers have found before. Your literature review should provide the evidence for your paper's argument: "This is what's been found before, therefore, here's why my argument makes sense."

With a literature review, you want to do more than just summarize what's been found before. This is not an annotated bibliography or a series of article summaries. Instead you want to integrate and synthesize the previous findings. The paragraphs should be organized by topic; they should not be organized by article. In general, each paragraph should include information from more than one source. Of course, you'll also want to use transitions between your paragraphs so there is a good flow of ideas.

Folks who are just starting out with scholarly writing often struggle with organizing their literature by topic. The key is to ask yourself what the major points are that you need to make, and make sure you have at least a paragraph for each.

For example, let's say you were writing a paper about whether Gender and Age are related to differences in Anxiety Symptoms. You'd then want several paragraphs that support why that's an important topic and why those variables make sense. So, you might have four paragraphs in your literature review:

1) A paragraph about what your sources say about why knowing about Anxiety Symptoms is important.
2) A paragraph about what your sources say about different factors that are related to Anxiety Symptoms.
3) A paragraph about what your sources say about how Gender is related to Anxiety Symptoms.
4) A paragraph about what your sources say about how Age is related to Anxiety Symptoms.

It's important to paraphrase the findings from your sources. APA Style introductions should almost never have direct quotes. You should stay away from including too much information from a single source. It's important to paraphrase the source's relevant findings and conclusions—you usually don't need to describe the details of their method or their statistical analyses.

When considering what information from the sources to include, you want to ask yourself what about this source will help make my argument? Do their conclusions support why your topic is important? Then that's what you should include. Do they examine the same variables you are examining but in a different way? Then you should include an explanation of how they examined the variables so you can explain how your study is different. Do they use a specific experimental design that you want to also use? Then that's what should be included from that source. Different sources will strengthen your argument in different ways, so the type of information you use from each source, and even how much information you use from each source will vary.

All information that comes from another source must include an in-text citation. The general structure for an in-text citation is to include the author's last name and the year the source was published. There are two broad ways we use in-text citations.

Sometimes we use parenthetical citations, where we use parentheses to separate the in-text citation from the rest of the sentence, typically at the end of the sentence. For example, this is a parenthetical citation (DeCicco & Dasch-Yee, 2020).

Other times the in-text citation is part of the sentence; this is called a narrative citation. For example, DeCicco and Dasch-Yee (2020) demonstrate how to use a narrative citation in this sentence. Either is fine to use (in fact, it's probably best to vary which one you use). It is just important to note the slightly different format for each.

Author Number	Parenthetical Citation	Narrative Citation
One Author	(DeCicco, 2020)	DeCicco (2020)
Two Authors	(DeCicco & Dasch-Yee, 2020)	DeCicco and Dasch-Yee (2020)
Three or More Authors	(DeCicco et al., 2020)	DeCicco et al. (2020)

You want to vary your writing style throughout the literature review. You want to avoid starting each sentence with an author's last name. For example, avoid this:

DeCicco (2020) found this finding. Dasch-Yee (2020) found this finding in a different population. McDonald (2020) found a different finding. Whittington's (2020) finding was similar to McDonald's finding.

Instead, you might write it like this:

This finding is really important (DeCicco, 2020). Others found a similar finding in a different population (Dasch-Yee, 2020). However, not everyone agrees. McDonald (2020) and Whittington (2020) both found a different finding.

As much as possible, the sources used in your literature review should be primary sources. Primary sources are those where the author writing the source is the same person who did the research. Primary sources describe findings from a research study for the first time. Secondary sources—that summarize many research findings together—should be used sparingly.

After the literature review, you should have a paragraph about the current paper you are writing. In this paragraph, you want to describe how your paper is expanding on the literature review to find something new. In this paragraph, you should:

1) Describe your research question (what is your paper trying to answer?).
2) Describe your variables—what are the specific factors you are looking at? If you have an experiment, be sure to explain what the independent variable is (the cause) and what the dependent variable is (the effect).
3) Explain how your paper is different from what's been done before. Sure, your paper is building on the literature review, but your paper should have a unique spin—explain it here.
4) State your hypothesis. Based on the literature review, what is your educated guess for the answer to your research question?

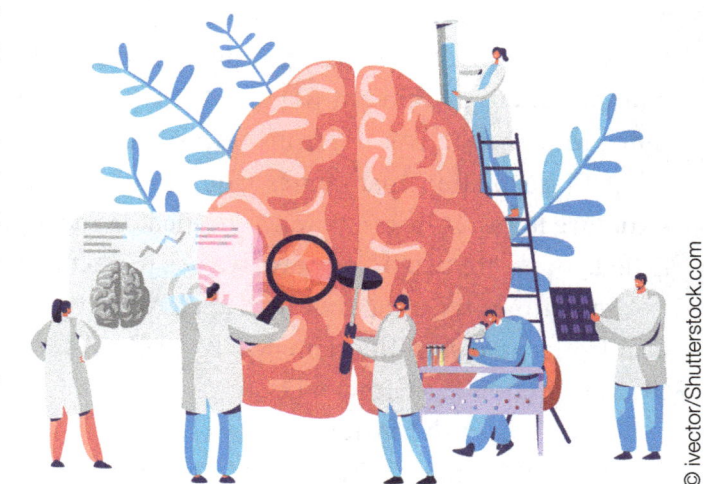

Method (Professional Paper Only)

The purpose of the method section is to describe the most critical components of how the study was conducted. The method section begins immediately after the introduction section, with the word method centered and in bold. The only circumstance where the method would begin on a new page would be if the word method is at the bottom of the previous page. The word method is a level 1 heading, followed by a participants section which is a level 2 heading. If you are writing a paper that involves animals instead of human participants, you would instead use the word subjects. The word participants (or subjects) should begin on the next line (double spaced after the word method) and is bolded. For example:

Method

Participants

Participants included 108 students from a small liberal arts college…

The participants section should cover important demographic information collected about the sample, such as but not limited to gender and age. Other inclusion or exclusion criteria should also be discussed in this section, as well as how participants were recruited, and if they were compensated or volunteers. The participants section should also include any additional information that helps a reader to understand the composition of the sample used in the study.

Materials

The second level 2 heading is the materials section, which should be presented in the same way as the participants section above. In this section you will *describe* the materials used in the study. It is important to note that you will **not discuss what participants did** with the materials, but rather describe what each material contains. The materials section may include several level 3 or level 4 headings to delineate multiple parts or components of a study. Some examples of materials could include questionnaires, stimuli, equipment, and other experiment-related materials. This section is expected to be detailed enough so that someone else would be able to replicate your study. This would include the size of a computer monitor, a discussion of the types of questions on a questionnaire, and the scale/response format that is presented.

Procedure

The last level 2 heading is the procedure section, which as the name suggests discusses the step-by-step procedures that participants are asked to perform. This section begins with signing a consent form and ends with debriefing the participant. Here it is important to note that since you described all of the details related to each of the materials participants were exposed to in the study, they just need to be mentioned here and not discussed in detail. If stimuli are presented or participants are asked to wait before performing the next task, it is important to provide how much time the participants needed to wait and how long stimuli are presented for. After designing your study this is typically one of the earlier sections you should be able to complete before you have completed data collection.

Results (Professional Paper Only)

The results section varies from experiment to experiment based on the design of the study. The results section should immediately follow the method section, with the word Results as a level 1 heading centered and in bold. The text for the results section would start double spaced and tabbed once as a regular paragraph. Here we will outline some of the basics to consider when writing a results section.

- The statistical symbols (F, t, r, etc.) are always written in italics.
- The p for a p value is always written in italics.
- There is always a space between operators. Operators include $<$ $>$ and $=$.
- Figures or tables that present results or help support the results should be cited within this section.

One of the most important things to remember about this section is that it only reports the data. There should **NOT** be any of the following as this should be done in the discussion section:

Interpretation
Suggestions for future research
Explanations about why a result did not support hypotheses
Explanations about why a result did support hypotheses

Though it is possible that you may have subsections and other level headings, this again varies based on the design of the study. All results sections have the word Results at the top of the section, centered and in bold; however, the content that follows typically varies from study to study based on the statistical analyses that the study needs to perform.

Discussion (Professional Paper Only)

The Discussion is then the section where you explain and interpret what you found in the Results. The Discussion should immediately follow the Results, with Discussion as a level 1 heading that is centered and in bold.

The discussion should include:

An explanation of your findings—Here is where you explain why you think the results came out the way they did. It is helpful to connect this explanation to what's been found in previous studies. Are these results a logical extension of what's been found before? Are these results surprising or in contrast with what's been found before? Use in-text citations (like you did in the Introduction) to make connections to previous studies.

Conclusions/implications about your findings—Here is where you explain the take-home message from your study. Why do these results matter? How could people use these results in real-world situations?

Limitations—Here is where you explain what your study was lacking. For example, did you have a small sample size? Did you only conduct your study with a specific group of people, like college students? However, you want your limitations to go beyond these two commonly mentioned limitations. Think about factors that perhaps limit the generalizability of your results or perhaps limit your ability to make firm causal conclusions.

Future directions—Finally, here is where you should discuss how future researchers should expand on your study or how future studies could improve on your study. What's the logical next step in this line of research? Should this topic be studied in different populations or different settings? Is there another type of research design that would allow for a different understanding? Is there another set of variables that should be considered or included?

References (Professional Paper and Student Paper Required)

The references section is where you should list all the sources used in your paper. The list of references should be alphabetized by the first author's last name. APA Style is very specific about how those references should be formatted. All references should have a hanging indent. That means the first line of the reference should be flush left, and all other lines should be indented. To do this, you need to make sure you can view the ruler at the top of the document. Then, slide the tabs so the first line is flush left and the other lines are indented. In Microsoft Word you can also highlight your entire references section, right click and use the paragraph option. In that new small window a special tab will come up. In there you can select hanging indent. Formats for common source types include the following:

Journal Article

Author, A. A., Author, B. B., & Author, C. C. (year). Title of article. *Title of Periodical, xx*(x), xx–xx. https://doi.org/xx.xxxxxxxxxx

Kong, L. L., Allen, J. J. B., & Glisky, E. L. (2008). Interidentity memory transfer in dissociative identity disorder. *Journal of Abnormal Psychology, 117*(3), 686–692. https://doi.org/10.1037/0021-843X.117.3.686

Book

Author, A. A., Author, B. B., & Author, C. C. (year). *Title of book.* Publisher Name.

Ingram, R. E., Miranda, J., & Segal, Z. V. (1998). *Cognitive vulnerability to depression.* Guilford Press.

Chapter in an Edited Book

Author, A. A., Author, B. B., & Author, C. C. (year). Title of chapter. In E. E. Editor (Ed.), *Title of book* (pp. xx–xx). Publisher Name.

Hammen, C. (2001). Vulnerability to depression in adulthood. In R. Ingram & J. Price (Eds.), *Vulnerability to psychopathology: Risk across the lifespan* (pp. 226–257). Guilford Press.

Online Source

Author, A. A., Author, B. B., & Author, C. C. (year, month date). *Title of work.* Site Name. https://xxxxxxx

Avila, Y., Cai, W., Harvey, B., Love, J., Lutz, E., Leeds Matthews, A., & Taylor, K. (2020, September 21). *What we know about coronavirus cases in K-12 schools so far.* New York Times. https://www.nytimes.com/interactive/2020/09/21/us/covid-schools.html

Supplemental Information: Tables, Figures, and Appendices

Tables, figures, and appendices appear in that order following the references section. Each table, figure, and appendix receive their own page. Tables, figures, and appendices are not required for either professional or student papers, but figures and tables are commonly used in professional papers. Tables and figures have a similar format in that the word Table or Figure appear at the top left in bold, with a description of the table or figure double spaced below the word Table or Figure. Each table and figure should be numbered, as shown below. The table or figure then appears below and centered on the page.

FIGURE 1

Mean Anxiety Scores By Age Group

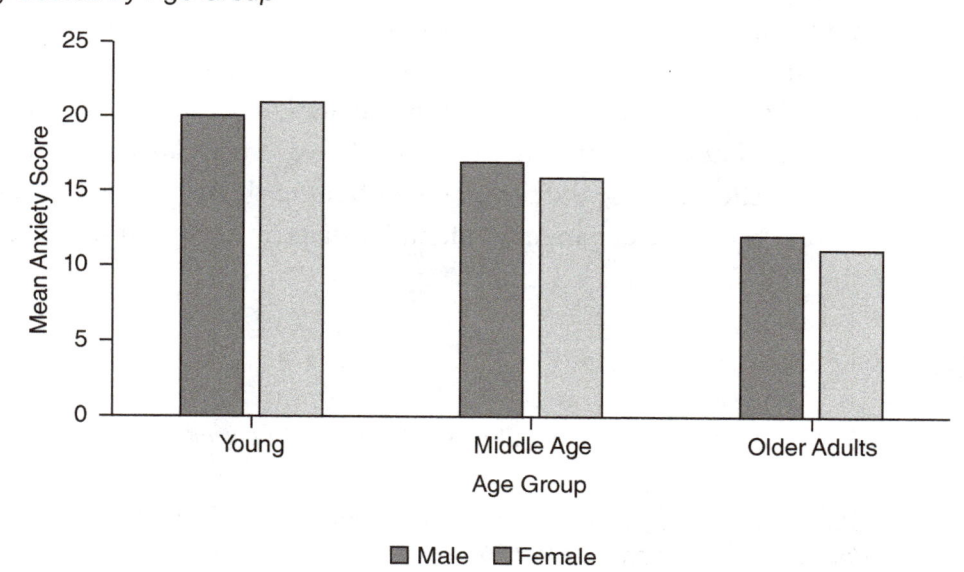

It is important to note that when considering whether to include a table or figure, you think about whether the table or figure provides critical information to help supplement your paper. Additionally, each table and figure that is included in your paper must be referenced in the text of your paper.

Appendices have a slightly different format, in that the word **Appendix** is bold and centered and uses letters instead of numbers. Therefore, the first appendix would be **Appendix A**. Appendices are used for the information that may not fit for a figure or table format. For example, you may have stimuli that were used in your experiment or other artifacts that were used and are important to communicate to your reader.

Final Words

When writing any type of paper, it is important to have the ability to go back, revise, edit, and then revise and edit again. Whether it is a professional paper or student paper, ensuring that you have time to revise and edit is an important step in improving your writing skills. In this process, having a peer edit your paper is also helpful, especially if a rubric is available for your assignment. Use the rubric to score your paper and ensure you are meeting all of the important points. Finally, writing is like a muscle, the more you work on it, the stronger it will get!

APA Professional Paper Checklist

Title Page
- ☐ Running head
- ☐ Page number 1
- ☐ Title
- ☐ Affiliation

Abstract
- ☐ Abstract in bold and centered
- ☐ Text left justified
- ☐ Keywords in italics; 3 to 5 keywords in regular font
- ☐ Begins on page 2

Introduction
- ☐ Title in bold and centered
- ☐ Begins on page 3

Method
- ☐ Method in bold and centered
- ☐ Immediately follows introduction
- ☐ Includes level 2 headings of Participants, Materials, and Procedure

Results
- ☐ Results in bold and centered
- ☐ Immediately follows method

- ❑ Check formatting for statistical values (e.g., *p*'s and statistical symbols)
- ❑ Tables and figures are referenced if included

Discussion
- ❑ Discussion in bold and centered
- ❑ Immediately follows results

References
- ❑ References in bold and centered
- ❑ Begins on new page
- ❑ Hanging indent
- ❑ Alphabetical order based on first author's last name
- ❑ Check each reference for specific APA formatting requirements

Tables, Figures, Appendices
- ❑ Each begins on a new page
- ❑ Present all tables, then all figures, then appendices
- ❑ Make sure each table, figure, or appendix is referenced in your paper
- ❑ Check each for their respective APA formatting requirements

General Guidelines
- ❑ Double spaced throughout
- ❑ 1" Margins
- ❑ Times New Roman size 12 font, Ariel size 11

APA Student Paper Checklist

Title Page
- ❑ Title
- ❑ Page number 1
- ❑ Name, Affiliation, Course, Instructor and Date

Introduction
- ❑ Title in bold and centered
- ❑ Begins on new page

References
- ❑ References in bold and centered
- ❑ Begins on new page
- ❑ Hanging indent
- ❑ Alphabetical order based on first author's last name
- ❑ Check each reference for specific APA formatting requirements

Tables, Figures, Appendices (Not required or common in student papers)
- ❏ Each begins on a new page
- ❏ Present all tables, then all figures, then appendices
- ❏ Make sure each table, figure, or appendix is referenced in your paper
- ❏ Check each for their respective APA formatting requirements

General Guidelines
- ❏ Double spaced throughout
- ❏ 1" Margins
- ❏ Times New Roman size 12 font, Arial size 11

Chapter 6
Writing as a Student Learning to Become a Teacher

Introduction

Teaching is one of the most important and essential jobs in our culture today—as they say, "if you can read this, thank a teacher." Teachers from preschool through 12th grade are readers, researchers, planners, writers, and documentarians of information about their specific subjects of expertise, about the field, and about their students. Although much of your time as a teacher will be as a presenter of information in one form or another, you will need to continue to develop and use your writing skills throughout your career in the teaching profession in order to perform the necessary tasks in all elements of the field. This might seem like an obvious point, but you are thinking about it from a very specific point of view. Right now, you are in college, reading this chapter, and writing for just about every class you take. This might not always be the case though, so preparing now for a life as an educator with skills as a writer is essential.

But here you are now, in college, reading this chapter, and writing for just about every class you take.

Throughout your college years, you will be asked to research, prepare, and present so much more than you ever wrote in high school. You need to be well prepared to express your thoughts in a variety of written forms. In this chapter, we will look at the forms of writing that future teachers produce for courses in the School of Education, as well as how developing your skills in those same forms of writing will prepare you for your career in teaching.

You are probably very familiar with some of the types of writing you are doing in college, because you have been doing them in some form for your entire school career. There will certainly be written tests and quizzes throughout your college years, just like there were in high school. Like it or not, these formative and summative types of writing show up again in college so that your professors have a variety of ways to assess what you know, what you need to know, and of course, what you learned. However, your professors know that tests and quizzes are not always the best way—or the

69

only way—to demonstrate knowledge and mastery of a topic. In addition, depending on the assignment, some ways of demonstrating knowledge simply work better!

Overview of Chapter

We will look at the demands of writing in the School of Education 1 year at a time, and fully define each type of writing that a preservice teacher needs to do in order to enter and complete the program.

Overview of Chapter:

I. Introduction
II. Overview of Chapter
III. Learning About the Field
   A. AADL
      1. Courses/Hours
IV. Writing in Education
   B. Class Notes You Will Really Use
   C. Experiences in the Field: Journals and Reflection Essays
   D. Writing to Curate Information: Annotated Bibliographies
V. The Teaching Connection
   E. Application to the School of Education: Passing the "Writing Test"
   F. Immersion in Content, Planning, and Application
   G. Teachers Stay Current
VI. Writing Lesson Plans
VII. Writing in Practicum
VIII. Writing IEP Goals and Behavioral Intervention Plans
IX. Writing Self-Assessments, Teaching Philosophy, and Your Mission Statement
   H. Writing Tips for Junior Year
   I. The Teaching Connection
   J. Senior Year: Elective Courses or Special Education Courses
   K. Student Teaching: Lessons, Reflections, and Units, Oh My
   L. Let Your Handbook Be Your Guide
X. Writing to Families as a Student Teacher
XI. Writing Tips for Senior Year
   M. Is That the Finish Line I See?
   N. Graduate School Is Inevitable: Write On
   O. Your First Years of Teaching
XII. Teachers Teach Writing, and Teachers Write
   P. Follow-Up Activities

Learning About the Field

It's a great feeling to enroll in those first education courses. Many students feel excited (and sometimes a little apprehensive) to begin the courses that launch their journey to become a teacher. Students working toward an Early Childhood PreK-4, PreK4/PreK-12 Special Education, or a stand-alone

PreK-12 Certification in Special Education all take the same courses in their first 2 years of study. These early courses give you the foundations of our field. They introduce you to child development, the history of the field of education and to inclusive education. (Certifications change to grade 12 from grade 8 on 12/21.)

Some Pennsylvania college students choose to seek certification in Early Childhood PK-4 so that they will be certified to teach preschool through grade 4. Many students choose the Dual Certification Program in PK-4/Special Education PK-12. This program enables students to apply for two certifications, whether or not they choose to become special education teachers. Becoming eligible for dual certification can be attained in the same number of college credits, but you will take specific courses in assessment and instructional design, behavior management, technology, transition to adult life, and teaching students with significant disabilities in place of the elective options in the Early Childhood PK-4 Certification. We will discuss that further in the junior and senior year sections.

Everyone Takes 'em: Adaptations and Accommodations for Diverse Learners a.k.a. the "AADL"

Courses/Hours

In 2007, the Commonwealth of Pennsylvania realized that no matter what type of classroom a student hoped to teach in, all teachers needed to recognize that classrooms contain a diversity of learners with a variety of learning support needs. The Commonwealth determined that our colleges and universities had to expose all teacher candidates to this reality and help them to be prepared. Holy Family met this important requirement by creating four courses called "Adaptations and Accommodations for Diverse Learners," AADL for short. Other colleges and universities provide similar courses, or embed the subject matter into course hours throughout their programs. Within the courses or course hours, all education students are introduced to best practices for teaching inclusively, better meeting the needs of students with disabilities and students who are English language learners. If you are a student who hopes to teach middle or high school Math, History, Biology, Social Studies grades 7-12 or Art in Kindergarten through grade 12, you will write in both your content major courses and in your education courses. As middle and secondary education students, you too are among the "all" students who take AADL courses.

Writing in Education

Class Notes You Will Really Use

Have you ever had to review your class notes for a paper or a test and realize you didn't understand what those notes mean now? You were writing or typing so much—or so little—that the notes don't make enough sense to use for writing or study. How can you write notes for a paper or test so that you can understand and use them later?

Consider using or adapting one or more of the many styles of writing notes that can help you as an undergraduate or graduate student, as a teacher, and even when you teach note taking to your students.

Here are four examples of ways to structure your notes for easier understanding of them later on:

The **Cornell Method** for note-taking was created at Cornell University in the 1950s. Divide your paper or document into two columns, with a narrow left-hand column containing the keywords, important terms, and the major concepts. The wider right column will contain the notes and descriptions you write for each term. At the bottom of the page, jot down a summary of the two columns in your own words, to help you remember your thoughts and associations about them.

Use the **Outline Method** to identify and classify your notes based on their levels of importance. You can use letters or numbers for your headings, and then put the supporting information below each particular heading in order of the degree of importance or relationship you feel that it has to the concept. If you are working on your computer, you may even choose to use your multilevel list function.

Despite this section being about writing, sometimes it's okay to aim to not write (as much). With the **Charting Method**, you create a matrix or spreadsheet with descriptors for your columns and/or rows, and then fill in the information in the appropriate spot. This style helps with coursework that emphasizes relationships between elements of information.

If you decide to write complete sentences during a lecture to retain your professor's words or terms, you are using the **Sentence Method**. Consider pairing this method with a more visual form of note-taking to provide balance and to help you to capture other elements of a discussion or lecture.

These models are just some examples of ways to organize what you hear into notes you can use and understand. You need to figure out a way to write your notes that works for you so they are clear and helpful when you need them for studying or for writing assignments.

Experiences in the Field: Journals and Reflection Essays

Several of your education classes will have a field experience, where you will be observing or working in classrooms. This time spent as a "fly on the wall" is a first intriguing foray into your future profession, as you observe teachers and students in diverse classroom settings. You will be responsible for a variety of written products in your observation experiences, such as **journals** and **reflection essays**. Pay careful attention to your instructor's requirements for papers based on observations. You will see these requirements and their point values in the **rubric** provided for any observation you complete. If you are tempted to ask your instructor "how many words does this have to be?", you may set their hair on fire, as the more important element is the coverage of the rubric requirements rather than the number of words it takes to cover them. It's not that it's a bad question, it is just not the most important question. Your instructors already know that for some, writing is joy, and for others, it feels like jumping out of a plane without a parachute every time you write. But write you must, and the more you write, the better and more comfortable you can become at writing. It's true.

At times, a reflection paper assignment may ask you to synthesize information from readings, class discussions, your class notes, observations, and other sources as required by your instructor to complement and support your reflection. Pay attention to how you are asked to cite your sources, and be sure to cite at least as many as the assignment requires. It is common in education to cite sources using the format of the **American Psychological Association, or APA**. Become familiar with the most recent version of the APA format early, as you will use it often in the coming years. Refer to APA guidelines section of this text or the Purdue OWL. Your University library is also a great resource for learning about APA and other style manuals. It is essential that you properly cite your sources when you draw information from any source, as you do not want to **plagiarize**, or take credit for someone else's writing or intellectual property. APA and other style manuals provide guidance on what constitutes plagiarism and how to avoid it in your writing.

Writing to Curate Information: Annotated Bibliographies

Another form of information gathering you will create in education courses is the **annotated bibliography**. An annotated bibliography can be a wonderful tool for you now and in the future. As you gather information about your assigned topic, you may find that you can return to the information collected in your bibliography to help you in other courses! Its contents will help you more deeply understand what you are asked to research because you are looking at several different publications about the assigned topic.

An annotated bibliography is a list of citations to books, articles, websites, and documents. Each citation is followed by a brief (usually about 150 words) descriptive and evaluative paragraph, the annotation. The purpose of the annotation is to inform the reader of the relevance, accuracy, and quality of the sources cited. (https://guides.library.cornell.edu/annotatedbibliography.) With an annotated bibliography, you not only get to gather materials of interest, you get to critique their quality and depth of coverage, too. And again, be sure that you are following the citation guidelines set by your instructor, APA, or otherwise. Look at the following citation example from the Purdue OWL (https://owl.purdue.edu/owl/general_writing/common_writing_assignments/annotated_bibliographies/annotated_bibliography_samples.html):

Ehrenreich, B. (2001). *Nickel and dimed: On (not) getting by in America*. Henry Holt and Company.

In this book of nonfiction based on the journalist's experiential research, Ehrenreich attempts to ascertain whether it is currently possible for an individual to live on a minimum-wage in America. Taking jobs as a waitress, a maid in a cleaning service, and a Walmart sales employee, the author summarizes and reflects on her work, her relationships with fellow workers, and her financial struggles in each situation.

An experienced journalist, Ehrenreich is aware of the limitations of her experiment and the ethical implications of her experiential research tactics and reflects on these issues in the text. The author is forthcoming about her methods and supplements her experiences with scholarly research on her places of employment, the economy, and the rising cost of living in America. Ehrenreich's project is timely, descriptive, and well-researched.

This sample annotation both summarizes and assesses the source that is being used in the citation. The first paragraph provides a summary of the content in the text, and the second paragraph provides an assessment of the source including its strengths, any biases that might be noted, the methods used, and the way the information was presented.

This part of the paragraph is sometimes followed by an explanation of how the source is of use to the research of the bibliographer, and how the source might be used to further their research or argument.

The Teaching Connection

Teachers are record-keepers. It is important to maintain anecdotal records about students in order to track their progress. This information will be collected formally and informally in order to help you better understand your student's strengths and needs. Clarity of expression will be important to your record keeping as well as to the information you will be sharing with school administration, teaching partners, and with families. The expectation of clarity of expression that your instructors have for your written assignments will be expected in your writing when you become a teacher.

Application to the School of Education: Passing the "Writing Test"

Students who hope to become teachers next must be accepted into their school of education teacher preparation program. There are several elements to the application for acceptance, including a strong grade point average (GPA), letters of recommendation, and passing of basic skills tests, including a writing test. It is a good idea to take all of the basic skills tests as early as possible in your college career. Study and test preparation guides and practice materials are available on the state education website, which links to the companies who provide and score the tests. Take the time to brush up on your writing skills before taking the test, as each test costs money and you want to avoid having to retake them to attain a passing score.

Freshman and sophomore year education courses are where you begin your journey toward becoming a teacher, and you will write on experiences both in and out of the college classroom. You will, of course, have mid-terms and final exams in some of your courses, so it will be important to be able to compose your thoughts in writing based on readings, experiences, and class discussions.

- Be sure to take notes in class so that you recall the important points of lectures and classroom activities; it is not enough to rely on what your professor may post on Canvas or any other learning management system, your memory, or what you highlight in a textbook. Your own notes need to support your professor's words and the text and help you to make sense of them after class.
- Writing more can make you a better writer. You will use the writing skills you gain in college to write as well as to teach writing during your teaching career.
- Take your basic skills tests early!
- Learn about the most current version of the style manual you are required to use, and avoid plagiarizing.

Immersion in Content, Planning, and Application

Once you have been accepted into the education program at your institution, you will dig more deeply into our field through courses in the teaching of content—math, science, social studies, language arts, and reading. You will also take more of your AADL courses. You will surely find areas of overlap between these courses and your content courses. Students are students, more alike than different, and their diversity of learning styles and learning needs is a given for which you must be prepared. As in your freshman and sophomore years, there may be written exams and assessments along the way, but you will be called to demonstrate your knowledge and understanding in ways that allow you to be creative within frameworks proven effective for optimal learning. Among these are the lesson plans, unit plans, and learning centers you will create in class. These experiences draw you closer to the actual writing responsibilities of a teacher.

Teachers Stay Current

As you prepare to enter the classroom, you will also review journal articles, website reviews, and present on educational research. It is important that you begin to see yourself as a lifelong learner, as there are new theories and techniques in education evolving all the time. Remember to review your instructor's assignment rubrics so that you are able to include all of the requirements of the assignment. Be sure to cite all sources in the assignment's required format (e.g., APA) so as not to be in danger of plagiarizing.

Writing Lesson Plans

Future teachers write them too.

As a preservice teacher, you will be introduced to **lesson plan** writing, a key skill to build now with support from your instructors, in preparation for your upcoming experiences in actual classrooms. You will be exposed to at least one lesson planning format in your college career, but all lesson planning formats have several elements in common. First and foremost, lesson plans must have **goals**, so that you identify the overall aim of your lesson. These goals are generally in the form of Common Core, District or State requirements or standards, so they are often already spelled out for you. Lesson plans must also contain **observable, measurable objectives**, written so that you can ultimately **assess** how well your students mastered what you were teaching. Your instructors in junior year will expect continued growth and development in your objective writing skills, which in turn help you to flesh out the steps of your lessons and assess your student's progress. One way to know that the lesson objective your write is observable and measurable is to make sure it includes your **audience**, the **behavior** they are to perform, and the *conditions* under which they will perform the behavior—think **ABC**! Your instructors will have other ways to help you structure your objectives, but they will always expect them to be observable and measurable.

What's the difference between a goal based on Common Core, State or District requirements, and a lesson plan objective? Why does a teacher need to include both? How can you tell the difference? One way is to think of a goal based on Common Core, State or District requirements as a broad outcome about the topic you are teaching based on what has been determined by the state or school district. Think of an objective as a step in making that goal happen, which will lead to a lesson that includes an introduction, learning activities, closure, and some way of assessing the student's learning. Key differences you will find between standards-based goals and an objective are the verbs used in each and their degree of specificity. For example, here's a goal from the PA Standards for a lesson plan for 2nd grade math (source HF Practicum Manual):

Specific Number: CC.2.3.3.A.2 Exact Wording: Use the understanding of fractions to partition shapes into parts with equal areas and express the area of each part as a unit fraction of the whole.

Here is a possible **objective** for that goal:

Students will be able to identify a fraction by comparing the number of shaded parts to the entire number of equal parts in the whole. Students will be able to represent a fraction using a picture or manipulatives.

Notice the difference in verb choice between the goal and the objective? Which one can you actually see happening? The verbs in the state goal, *understand* and *express*, are what you want the student to be able to do, but you can't really observe or measure if someone understands or expresses. The verbs in the objective, *compare* and *represent*, describe tangible ways in which the concept will happen—HOW the student will demonstrate that they understand or express, and what they will do to show it. Again, think "ABC," audience, behavior, and conditions as you write your lesson objective:

A: 2nd grade students
B: compare a fraction, represent a fraction
C: using a picture or manipulatives

Practice will improve your ability to write lesson objectives, which will ultimately improve your lessons. Observable, measurable objectives make it easier for you to visualize and ultimately write up the steps of your plan so that you can carry it out. Your instructors may advise you to write a lesson plan so clearly and completely that someone else could teach it if you weren't there! Below you will find a standard daily lesson plan template that you can follow in order to begin the lesson planning process.

Daily Lesson Plan Template			
Instructional Context			
Student's Name:			
Cooperating Teacher's Approval:		Date:	
Unit of Study:		Topic:	Grade:
Allocated Time:		Student Population:	
Instructional Focus			
Common Core, State Standards or District Requirements		Specific Number: Exact Wording:	
Instructional Objective Statement			
Assessment of Objective			
Estimated Time↓		**Instructional Elements/Procedure**	
		Engagement/Introduction:	
		Representation/Developmental Activities:	
		Expression/Closure:	
Teacher Materials:		**Student Materials:**	
Resources/References:			
Self-Assessment			
Following the delivery of your lesson, enter your reflections on its strengths and weaknesses here.			

Writing in Practicum

You will be placed in two practice teaching settings, a.k.a. Practicum, working one semester with younger students, the other with upper primary grade students for 1 day a week. This exposure will help you to more deeply understand the nature of classrooms, the responsibilities of the teacher, and your own aptitude for the art and science of teaching. You will write several lesson plans for your classes and for Practicum, and you will get to teach at least one of them each semester. You will also create at least one **Choice Project** in your Practicum as another way to learn about effective instructional practice. You and your cooperating teacher will coordinate this project, and the choice really is yours. It may be direct work with children, such as reading a story, or something creative, such as a bulletin board, learning game, or prop box, and the ability to communicate your plan in writing before its execution will be essential to its effectiveness.

Ideally, your Practicum will also serve as a preview of the more complex work of student teaching in senior year. Your lesson plans, Choice Projects, and all other written work will be evaluated by you as the writer, your supervisors, and your cooperating teachers according to a writing rubric such as the **PSSA Domain Rubric for Writing**. You will need to be conscientious and professional in your writing, attending to the following domain areas:

Focus: *The single controlling point made with an awareness of task (mode) about a specific topic.* In other words, state and clearly develop and support your selected topic throughout your writing.

Content: *The presence of ideas developed through facts; examples, anecdotes, details, opinions, statistics, reasons, and/or explanations.* In other words, carefully choose what information you will include to develop your topic fully.

Organization: *The order developed and sustained within and across paragraphs using transitional devices and including introduction and conclusion.* In other words, make your work accessible to your reader through the way you structure your written work. Introduce your topic, develop your topic, bring your reader to an understanding of the conclusion you want to reach. Even research has an element of storytelling to it!

Style: *The choice, use, and arrangement of words arrangement of words and sentence structures that create tone and voice.* In other words, think of your written work as another way of speaking to your reader. Develop a written style that fits the nature of the assignment, just as you probably have a spoken style that fits the formality or informality of the situation you are in.

Conventions: *Grammar, mechanics, spelling, usage, and sentence formation.* In other words, be sure you follow the rules of writing, such as good grammar, correct spelling, and well-formed sentences. When in doubt, run the spell and grammar check on your computer.

You may find it helpful to find a friend or family member who can proofread your work with an eye to any or all of the domains. Sometimes, especially after you have read your own work over and over, it is hard to see areas for revision or improvement. A friend, family member, or even the spell check, grammar check, and edit suggestions functions on your software can help you see what works well and what could be corrected or clarified.

Writing IEP Goals and Behavior Intervention Plans

Teachers must be prepared to support all the students in their classrooms, including those who require special education services. You will learn about Individual Education Plans (IEPs) and Behavior Intervention Plans (BIPs) through your coursework, especially if you decide to pursue a dual major in Special Education PK-12th grade and PreK-4. Teachers and other members of the school-based teams who work on IEPs and BIPs generate goals based on information such as observations, interviews, assessments, and data collection. It will be essential to write objectives for these plans that are observable and measurable so that progress can be assessed.

Writing Self-Assessments, Teaching Philosophy, and Your Mission Statement

Teachers improve their knowledge and skills through self-reflection as well as through research and practice. Throughout your coursework, you will be asked to look back as well as to look forward; looking back to write in assessment of your own performance on a task, in a group, or perhaps across a period of time. You will also be asked to look forward, to generate a personal philosophy or mission statement about your teaching. This is not a final document but one which will likely evolve as you deepen your knowledge and understanding of the field of education. Your philosophy and mission statement will guide you in creating a vision for your welcoming classroom of the not too distant future. This philosophy or mission begins by thinking and writing about the why and the how of creating that classroom. You will write about how to be that teacher whose classroom is accessible to all through your instructional style and method, your use of classroom space, your use of materials, and more. Your instructors will assist you in putting your vision into words that create a guiding "north star" for all you are learning and doing in classes and experiences in the field.

Writing Tips for Junior Year

Junior year will be two exciting and challenging semesters that can truly validate your career choice and prepare you to enter the classroom as a student teacher, and ultimately, as a teacher. For now:

- Remember to cite sources of the information you use in your writing in the format required by your instructor. Plagiarism is wrong, whether you mean to do it or not. It is also easy to prevent if you know how to give credit to your sources.
- Pay careful attention to the content of your objectives for lesson plans, and your goals and objectives for IEPs. Be sure that they are observable and measurable so that you can assess student progress.
- Carefully follow the rubric set by your instructor for all written assignments.
- Review the Manual you will be provided for Practicum for details and templates you will need for your placement.
- Pace yourself; your first written draft of any assignment should not be your final. Be prepared to revise your work, and give yourself enough time to do it.

The Teaching Connection

Lesson planning, the plan-full mindset that goes into even the most informal moments of instructional delivery, will become somewhat second nature to you as a teacher, but you are not to that point yet! As you learn the connection between assessment and the creation of goals and objectives, you will see that clarity makes for better teaching, and that you can easily assess student performance when you write objectives that are observable and measurable. Junior year is a learning laboratory. Next year, you will complete a semester of classwork and a semester of student teaching. The finish line is not too far away!

Senior Year: Elective Courses or Special Education Courses

Your last two semesters of college will consist of a final full-time semester of courses and a full semester of student teaching with one culminating course on families. The order of these semesters will depend on which certification you are seeking. You will encounter many of the same types of assigned writing as you did in your first 3 years of college, with an emphasis on special education issues if you pursue the dual major and elective courses if you seek certification in PreK-4. The difference is that by now your instructors will assume that your knowledge and the quality of your written work have developed to the point where you are ready to assume the professional duties of a student teacher. Their expectations are higher, so yours should be, too.

Student Teaching: Lessons, Reflections, and Units, Oh My.

Your student teaching semester will challenge you as no other semester. You will dress better because you are entering classrooms as a professional! You will spend much less time on campus because you are out in the field, teaching! You will become more a part of the culture of the school where you student teach and less of your university (we miss you already). This is a natural progression as you move ever closer to your career as an educator. Congratulations! Get a good night's sleep, eat breakfast, and take good care of yourself. You are about to be immersed in the life of a student teacher.

Let Your Handbook Be Your Guide

Student teachers write for both the classroom curriculum and for the course that is called student teaching. You will write lesson plans in the way that you have practiced writing in your courses and in Practicum, but they will be for a flesh and blood daily student audience. You will also propose and compose plans for a unit of study, in collaboration with your cooperating teacher and university supervisor.

A **unit plan** is a series of lessons generated around a topic area, for example, Pennsylvania Colonial Era History, and it is more comprehensive than just one lesson on a topic. You, now a student teacher, will create your unit to be taught over a span of time you will decide on with your cooperating teacher, and your topic can appear in any subject area or areas you choose. Math? Social Studies? Science? It's up to you and your cooperating teacher!

Holy Family University's Student Teaching Handbook provides a helpful description of units:

> Think of a unit of study as a set of integrated facts, concepts, skills and, perhaps, dispositions around a given topic. The unit is delivered as a set of sequenced lessons designed to move students from where they are to where you want them to be at the conclusion of the unit. Begin your planning by first identifying your intended learning outcomes for the unit and then design your summative assessment as a performance assessment. The performance assessment should require students to use their newly acquired knowledge, conceptual frameworks and skills. This will help cement their learning. Once you have created your summative assessment (which provides evidence of student understanding), plan backwards from this exercise to the series of lessons that will prepare students for success. (HF Student Teaching Handbook, 2019–2020)

You will probably feel a great sense of ownership of the content of your unit, as it represents conceptualizing and delivering instruction at the level of a professional educator.

The handbook associated with Student Teaching can be a tremendous resource to you as a student teacher, so read it carefully and refer to it as often as you need. Your field supervisor can help you navigate the requirements of this all-important semester, and your handbook includes templates and forms you will use to complete the elements of planning the school day as you assume more and more responsibility for the delivery of instruction to your students. You will probably not be surprised by some of the templates and format, but you may be surprised by how much more deeply you are involved with them as a student teacher. Your ability to write daily and eventually weekly plans, units, and your skills at organization, journaling, reflection papers, and self-assessments will be extremely important to you during your student teaching semester.

Writing to Families as a Student Teacher

Teachers must communicate with families throughout the school year. This communication can strengthen the relationship between you and the families of your students, which helps you to be a better teacher in the long run. Often, family communication looks like a letter home, an email, a newsletter, blog, or a class website in addition to face-to-face conferences and meetings. You will write to families to share information about the class, the school, the student, and other relevant topics. As a student teacher, you will have the opportunity to see examples of written communication with families, as well as to try some out yourself.

You may find that the first communication you will have with families is the writing of a letter of introduction of yourself as the new student teacher in their child's classroom. Families want to know who is working with their child, as students will begin to speak of you, the new face in the classroom, when asked "how was your day?" Use the letter of introduction to help families get to know you and why you are now a part of their child's life. Feel free to share relevant information about yourself, such as your major, your experience with children, why you want to become a teacher, and why you are excited to work with their child. Families will also enjoy learning about your interests and hobbies, since they make you an even more exciting addition to their child's day. You can find templates for your introduction letter online, but sometimes it works best to write from the heart. The students in your student teaching placement will hold a special place for you years after you leave. And you will hold a special place in theirs and that of their families, too. Below you will find a sample of this kind of a letter.

Hello 4th grade families!

My name is Ms. HW and I am so excited to be student teaching in your child's 4th grade classroom! I will be in your student's classroom until the end of April as a representative of Holy Family University. Currently, I am dual majoring in Early Education PK-4 and Special Education PK-8. Luckily, I know a lot about 4th graders since I coach 3rd/4th grade girls lacrosse in West Deptford, NJ! I have lived in New Jersey since I was born but have enjoyed my college career so far in Philadelphia! I look forward to getting to know more about your student in these upcoming months and cannot wait to share my love of teaching with this class.

Thanks,
Ms. HW

> **Fun Facts About Me!**
>
> <u>My pets:</u> 1 yorkie-poodle mix dog named Kenobi and 1 tea-cup yorkie named Sugar
>
> <u>Favorite color:</u> Purple
>
> <u>Favorite sports team:</u> Philadelphia Eagles
>
> <u>Favorite holiday:</u> Halloween
>
> <u>Hobbies:</u> Lacrosse, reading, exercising, cooking, and watching movies

Teachers also need to create goals and objectives for IEPs and BIPs in collaboration with support teams which include the child's family. You will be able to review these plans if there are students receiving special education supports and services in your classroom. Examining and helping to carry out IEPs and BIPs will help prepare you to eventually write or assist with the writing of goals and objectives yourself as a part of the student's support team.

Writing Tips for Senior Year

A final semester of coursework, and a semester of student teaching; welcome to senior year. You are familiar with the writing demands of your coursework by now, and the need to pace yourself, to follow assignment rubrics and to utilize the technical aspects of writing and source citation so that your communication is clear and professional.

Student teaching is the last time that your instructors in the field will "watch over you" as you begin to acclimate to the world of the professional educator. Your student teaching semester will combine academic requirements of you as still a student, with professional requirements of you as now an apprentice teacher.

- Read, review, and refer to your Student Teaching Handbook and the structure and forms it provides to help you structure your experience. You will be writing to reflect, to observe, and to self-assess. The more you become comfortable with writing is the better writer you can become, as well as the better writing teacher!
- You will write many lesson plans and a unit plan in student teaching, real sequences of activities by real classes of children. Remember that your objectives need to be observable and measurable so that you can assess your students.
- Follow the rubrics of your classes and your student teaching requirements.
- Pace yourself; teaching is filled with planning and preparation. You will take on more and more of the school day as a student teacher, so one lesson will transition to the next and the next.
- Learn about and try the types of written communication teachers frequently use to stay in

contact with families such as letters home, newsletters, emails, blogs, and classroom websites. Take advantage of opportunities to write under the guidance of your cooperating teacher and field supervisor.

Is That the Finish Line I See?

Congratulations on completing student teaching! Now what? Certification tests and licensure? Graduate school? A teaching job? All of the above?

As you consider your next steps, remember that the university is still watching over you. Cover letter and resume writing services are available through the Career Development Center, as well as information about career fairs, job openings, and other professional opportunities. Experts will work with you to prepare a strong cover letter to introduce yourself and your skills that is tailored to the needs of each school to which you apply. Realize that your cover letters must be targeted for each application. Generic cover letters attached to cookie cutter resumes do not get you a job. Prepare to research the job before you write to apply for it so that your application has a real chance to get you an interview and ultimately a teaching job.

Graduate School Is Inevitable: Write On

Maintaining your certification means continuing your education. Your application to graduate school will likely include an essay which will be read by those who are considering your credentials. Your written workload as a grad student will be considerably heavier than your undergraduate years, and it is possible that you will be working full-time alongside pursuing your Master's degree.

Your First Years of Teaching

Teachers Teach Writing, and Teachers Write

If it can be said that "if you can read this, thank a teacher," perhaps for the sake of closure we can alter the phrase a little to say "if you can write about it, thank a teacher." Teachers teach writing, through direct instruction in the mechanics of writing, and giving students exposure an opportunity to express themselves and learn through exposure to different types of writing assignments. Teachers teach writing indirectly, by modeling writing with students and modeling a love and enjoyment of every chance to write. Teachers allow students to be writers as well as editors and critics, teaching them to value the feedback of others, including their classmates, as they write to communicate their experiences. Teachers help all students see themselves as writers, and give them whatever tools and technologies they need to be writers. Teachers help students pay attention to the world around them, write about it, and enjoy the experience.

First, however, it helps if you as a teacher see yourself as a writer. It is time for you to identify as a writer, even a reluctant one, because you have already done so much writing throughout your own education. Now, as a teacher, you have the opportunity to expand your writing to reach even more readers than you did in school—to reach your students, their families, your school and community, and to reach your colleagues in the field. Find new places to be a writer as an e-mailer, as a blogger, in the creation of a class newsletter or website, even in writing about the experience of being a teacher. Write for your reader, write for yourself, but write and write. Read and learn from the writing of other educators, as no one knows the field better than someone who is in it.

Someone like you.

Follow-Up Activities

1. Which three words would be good choices for writing observable, measurable objectives?

   _____ learn   _____ compare   _____ locate

   _____ calculate   _____ understand   _____ appreciate

2. Which of the following could be defined as an observable and measurable objective?
   a. Third grade students will learn about fractions using manipulatives.
   b. Using rulers or measuring tape, second grade students will measure four objects to the nearest ½ inch.
   c. Students will understand the First Amendment to the U.S. Constitution.
3. Review the contents of the American Psychological Association's APA Style Website at https://apastyle.apa.org/ and answer the following:
   a. What is the most current edition of the APA Publication Manual?
   b. Find and list at least three areas on the site that can be of help to you in your writing.
4. Review university library writing supports at https://academicwriter-apa-org.holyfamily.idm.oclc.org/6/. Make a note for yourself describing how each section can help you in your class writing assignments.
   a. Learn:
   b. Reference:
   c. Write:

References

- **Cult of pedagogy**
- (https://www.education.pa.gov/Documents/Teachers-Administrators/Certification%20Preparation%20Programs/Framework%20Guidelines%20and%20Rubrics/Accommodations%20and%20Adaptations%20and%20ELL%20Program%20Framework%20Guidelines.pdf
- (https://miamioh.instructure.com)
- HF Practicum and Student teaching handbooks
- (https://guides.library.cornell.edu/annotatedbibliography)
- (https://apastyle.apa.org/).
- **https://www.nais.org/magazine/independent-teacher/spring-2014/teachers-write/**
- https://www.edweek.org/tm/articles/2019/07/30/why-teachers-should-write.html
- https://medium.com/@heinemann/why-teachers-need-to-write-for-the-public-b44ac3b5083f
- https://www.theatlantic.com/national/archive/2012/09/the-best-writing-teachers-are-writers-themselves/262858/

Chapter 7
A Guide to Writing History Papers

Introduction

So, you have a writing assignment in your history class? It may be a short essay, a research paper, or a book review. Perhaps you are a history major, eager to explore a topic you have always wondered about. Just as likely, however, you are majoring in a different area altogether. You may be wondering why you have to write a history paper when this will never help you in your future career in nursing, marketing, psychology, or criminal justice. Learning to write a history essay or paper, though, can help you in your future career by sharpening your skills in researching, organizing, logical thinking, supporting ideas with evidence, and writing. A recent history graduate of my acquaintance got a job as an IT project manager in part because his boss recognized that writing lots of history papers had given him the skills in research, organizing, and writing that a project manager has to have.

This chapter on writing history papers is designed to help you to enhance your skills, to write better essays and papers, and perhaps even to raise your GPA. The chapter will consider types of writing assignments you may have to do, explain how to do historical research, discuss how to organize and to write essays and papers and how to revise them, and provide examples of how to document the sources you use.

The purpose of writing, as of speaking, is to communicate. If a person reading your paper does not get your message, you have not successfully communicated your ideas. So, as a writer, you have two tasks: to decide in your own mind what you want to say, and to find the most effective way to communicate your message to the reader.

Overview of Chapter:

I. Introduction
II. Types of Writing Assignments
   A. Short Essays
   B. Research Essays
      1. Primary and Secondary Sources
      2. Taking Notes as You Research
      3. Writing the Paper
   C. Book Reviews
   D. Annotated Bibliography
      1. Footnotes and Endnotes
      2. Chicago Style Bibliographic Guidelines
   E. Avoiding Plagiarism
   F. Revising Your Paper

Types of Writing Assignments

The three typical writing assignments you will encounter in history courses are the short essay, the longer research paper, and the book review. In upper level history courses, you may also have to write an annotated bibliography.

Short Essays

In introductory level courses, you will most often encounter the short essay, which can appear in various forms, including as a formal paper, as a take-home exam, or as an in-class essay. The short essay may be anywhere from one to five pages, and you will typically have a directed question such as "What factors help explain the Islamic expansion and conquest?" or "Compare and contrast the Populist and Progressive movements in terms of goals and achievements." You might be given a document such as the Code of Hammurabi or the Emancipation Proclamation to read and to analyze. When writing the short essay, the most important thing to do is to answer the question that is asked. If you are asked to compare the Populist and Progressive movements, but you write only about the Populists, you cannot expect to get a passing grade.

If you are encountering the short essay as a take-home exam or paper, you will need, first, to gather the required materials. If you have to analyze a section of the Code of Hammurabi, you will need a copy of that Code. You will also need your textbook, class notes, and any PowerPoint or assigned film clip or other relevant material. Read through the materials slowly and carefully, highlighting and annotating (writing notes in the margin) relevant material, and writing notes to yourself on paper or on a device about information that you think should be included in the essay.

You can follow similar steps in preparing to write essays for in-class exams. Your instructor may have given you a list of possible essay questions or a list of topics. In the case of the latter, it will be your responsibility to think about potential essay questions, and then to prepare to answer these questions in the same way: by gathering materials, highlighting and annotating, and taking notes on important information to put in your answer.

When you have pulled together the needed information, organize it in an outline that will help you to answer the question. Look back at the question you have been asked to answer: do you have enough information to answer the question completely, or is there an area that is weaker and needs more development? If so, go back and do more reading and note-taking until you are satisfied.

You will now need to develop a thesis: what are you arguing in the paper? Perhaps your argument is that "The Arabs' need for land, the weakened condition of surrounding Christian empires, and the unifying role of the Muslim religion combined to enable Islamic expansion and conquest," or that "The Populists and Progressives shared many social, political and economic goals, but the Progressives were better able to achieve these goals because they had a broader base of support in American society."

Every essay must be organized around a thesis, which is an argument that you are trying to prove. When you have developed that thesis, you must support it with evidence, and then refer back to the thesis in the paper's conclusion. In the typical five-paragraph essay, your introductory paragraph will contain a thesis, your next three paragraphs will provide evidence to support the thesis, and your last paragraph will conclude the paper, referring back to the thesis. You will also need to proofread the essay and, if it is a paper, provide correct citations for any sources you have used. More on citation follows later in this chapter.

Research Essays

For research papers, which may be anywhere from 8 to 25 or more pages in length, your professor may assign you a topic or, more likely, allow you to choose a topic within the parameters of the course. You will want to choose a topic that is narrow enough that you can address it in a substantive way in a research paper, but that is not so narrow that it is difficult to find any information at all about it. For ideas for papers, you can look at a list of possible topics provided by the professor, or look at topics covered in the syllabus, or look at the indexes at the ends of any books that have been assigned for the course. If the instructor says he or she is happy to talk with you about ideas for papers, you should probably talk to the professor.

As you begin to do research on your topic, you will need to refine it into a narrower research question that you can answer. If your general topic of inquiry is the role of women in the American Civil War, you might narrow the topic down to the question did female soldiers make a significant contribution to the northern army in the American Civil War? If you are researching the Irish independence movement, you might consider the question did the violence of the Irish Republican Army in the 1910s and 1920s advance or retard the cause of Irish independence?

After you have chosen a research question, you will need to research it. It is certainly tempting just to use the internet, but do not succumb to that temptation. Not all information on the internet is equally reliable; anyone can put up a .com or a .org site and fill it with information that may or may not be correct. What may look like a great site may actually just be a high school freshman's term paper—and one on which the student received a D at that! If you use the internet, it is best to rely on sites that have as their suffix .gov or .edu; information on those sites is more likely to have been verified and to be correct. (Even on these sites, however, you can find pages that have more or less accurate information, especially on .edu sites. Some faculty put their students' uncorrected work up on .edu websites, so you have to be careful.)

Wikipedia is a .org website, and because it is a Wiki, anyone may edit the information, and so it is not too reliable. However, some Wikipedia entries do have good endnotes and/or bibliographies that may steer you toward sources that are helpful.

To use websites effectively, you need to evaluate them. Can you tell who the author is, and whether the author has academic qualifications or is associated with a university? Does the author seem qualified to write on the topic, or does the author say, straight out, that s/he has no training in this area but has put the site up just because s/he is interested in the topic? Note that someone's ethnic heritage does not qualify the person to be a scholarly authority on a topic. What is the purpose of the website? Is this page scholarly, or a personal webpage, or a commercial site? Is the information on the page balanced and objective, or biased and subjective, or a little of both? Is there a way to communicate with the webmaster if you notice anything that is incorrect or if you want more information? Has the webpage been updated recently? (Some websites with historical information may not be updated often; for example, a .gov webpage about the architect who built the US Capitol building in the 1800s is unlikely to need frequent updating.)

Primary and Secondary Sources

When you retrieve information from the internet, it is best to focus on using primary sources; primary sources are documents *from* the past such as diaries and letters, census records, speeches and documents produced by government officials, and newspaper articles, to give a few examples. These kinds of documents allow you to build your own historical arguments. Many governments, universities, and historical societies sponsor websites with primary source information; for example, the U.S. Library of Congress (Library of Congress Digital Collections), Yale University (The Avalon Project), and Fordham University (Internet History Sourcebooks Project) all have very helpful databases of primary source documents.

Secondary sources are also available on the internet. Secondary sources are documents *about* the past written by people who did not personally experience the events they are writing about. A book written in 1865 about the Mexican-American War of 1845–1846 by an historian who did not experience the war firsthand could be just as much a secondary source on that topic as a book published in 2020 would be (although if it was a first-person account of the experiences of someone who fought in the war, it would be a primary source). Secondary sources generally reflect the points of view of their authors as they try to interpret and explain the past, and that is just fine; everyone has a point of view, including you. You just need to be aware of the point of view of the writer so you can understand what the author may have included in the account, and what the author may have left out. When you use secondary sources, you need to know if the author is knowledgeable about the topic. This is why .coms may not be reliable sources: you do not know anything about the person who created the website. On the other hand, if you are using a website sponsored by the Library of Congress (.gov) or PBS (.org), you can have some confidence that they will have protected their reputations by using knowledgeable people to write any secondary source information that appears on their websites.

Journals, which are published by universities and by scholarly or professional organizations, are a very good source of secondary information. Journals always identify the academic affiliations of the authors of their articles. For historians, JSTOR, a database of journals in the social sciences, is a valuable resource. Another database of journal articles, Academic Search Ultimate, includes both scholarly journals and commercial trade publications, so you need to be careful of which sources you choose to use. Scholarly journals are more reliable because they are refereed; this means that before any article is published, three or four experts review the article independently to determine if the information is reliable and the conclusions reached are sound. A trade publication, on the other hand, does not use the same sort of rigorous review process and so mistakes may creep in. Thus, if you want to learn about the early settlement of Jamestown, Virginia, choose an article in the *William and Mary Quarterly* rather than *Smithsonian Magazine*.

The university library is good place to check for secondary sources. If you choose books that have been published by university presses (Oxford, the University of North Carolina, Columbia, etc.), you will know that, before publication, these book manuscripts have been reviewed by at least three or four scholars known as being authorities on the book's topic; this does not eliminate mistakes, but at least it minimizes them. After publication, these books are again reviewed by scholars in the field; university librarians consult these book reviews before the books are purchased for the library.

University librarians can help you to do advanced searches, using the best search terms, to locate books on your topic. When you do find a book's call number, look also at the books on the shelves around the book that you need; you may see that other nearby books also address the topic of your paper. If the university's library does not have a particular book on its shelves, a librarian can help you to request a book through Interlibrary loan; it generally takes just a couple of days for the book to arrive on campus and then you can check it out as you would any other library book.

Taking Notes as You Research

As you read through the primary source documents, journal articles, and books on your topic, you will need to take notes on the information you are reading. When taking notes, try to put the information into your own words. Read a passage, write a summary, and then go back to see that you have explained the information correctly and to check whether you need to add anything more. Summarizing the information in your own words as you research will help you to avoid problems with plagiarism as your write.

If you choose not to put the information into your own words as you take notes, make sure that you make clear in your notes that you are using exact quotes (use quotation marks), and do quote the words exactly, neither shortening the sentence nor adding in additional words.

Whether you are summarizing the information in your own words, or copying the words exactly, record carefully the source of your information. You do not want to have to track down which book or website a particular sentence came from at 11 pm just before a paper is due. Write down the name of the author, the title, the webpage if there is one and the date you looked at the source, and also the page number(s) of the article or book where you found the information.

Writing the Paper

After you have done a significant amount of research, review your notes and think back to your research question: did female soldiers make a significant contribution to the northern army in the American Civil War? Or, did the violence of the Irish Republican Army in the 1910s and 1920s advance or retard the cause of Irish independence? Now it is time for you to write a thesis, based on the evidence that you have amassed, that you can defend in your paper. For example: "By serving in a variety of roles, from nurses, to spies, to officers in the Civil War, female soldiers made a significant contribution to the Union Army in the American Civil War." Or, "The guerrilla warfare sparked by the Irish Republican Army made the island seem ungovernable to the British government, causing the Crown to agree to the establishment of an Irish Free State comprising 26 Irish counties in 1922."

When you have developed a thesis statement, you can start to arrange your evidence in a supporting outline. (Or, you may choose to write the outline first, using it to help develop your thesis statement.) Arrange your ideas to make a logical argument. Think about what information you need to include, and in what order it makes the most sense. For example, if your thesis is: "The guerrilla warfare sparked by the Irish Republican Army made the island seem ungovernable to the British government, causing the Crown to agree to the establishment of an Irish Free State comprising 26 Irish counties in 1922," it would make sense to develop one section of the paper on the guerrilla warfare of the IRA, a second section on Great Britain's attempts to rein in the violence, and a third section on the decision that Britain made to establish the Irish Free State of 26 counties.

As you write an outline, keep close track of the sources you are using for your information; it will make it much easier for you, later on, to write footnotes and endnotes for the paper.

As you write your outline, you may decide that you need to revise your thesis statement. For example, while your initial thesis may have been that by serving in a variety of roles, women soldiers made a significant contribution to the Civil War, as you write your outline it may strike you that there were only about 250 documented examples of female soldiers in a war in which millions of male soldiers fought, and your thesis needs to reflect this: "While female soldiers served in a variety of roles, from nurses, to spies, to officers in the Union Army, their numbers were so small that one cannot argue that they made a significant contribution to the northern army in the American Civil War."

Once you have outlined your paper, you are ready to start writing. Your paper's title should be brief, just a few words, but it should convey the main ideas of your paper. The most important paragraph you will write will be your first. Your introduction should state your thesis, and also be interesting enough to "hook" the reader on your paper. After you give your evidence in the next few pages of your essay, you need to finish with a conclusion. Your conclusion should briefly summarize how you have proven your thesis. The conclusion should not contain new evidence, but it can give readers an idea of new areas for study.

As you review your evidence for the paper, you may find that there is also counter-evidence that argues against your thesis. Rather than ignore the counter-evidence, include it in the paper, while explaining why it does not undermine your thesis. For example, you may have run across a testimonial by a Civil War soldier stating that the bravest soldier and surest shot in his unit turned out to be a woman. You can acknowledge this woman's superior contribution to the war while pointing out that this was just one person, in one unit, in an army that numbered in the millions, and so her contribution, while significant to her unit, is not sufficient to demonstrate that women who served as soldiers overall made a significant contribution to the war.

Once you have written your conclusion, congratulations are in order, because now you are done—with your *first* draft! Go over your draft, add, delete, and clarify your sentences, rearrange paragraphs, correct grammar and spelling. Spelling and grammar are important. Poor spelling and grammar can prevent effective communication; therefore, instructors will make note of and correct your spelling and grammar mistakes, and they will affect your grades. You would not want to turn in a poorly written memo to your boss at work, and faculty do not want to receive a poorly written paper. It is helpful to write the first draft early enough that you can set it aside for a few days so you can look at the draft with fresh eyes. After you have gone over a few drafts, ask someone else to read your paper before you turn in your final draft.

You will also need to provide correct citations for the paper; more on citation follows later in this chapter.

Book Reviews

In middle or high school, you may have had to write a book summary, in which you explained the plot of a book and probably concluded with a statement of whether or not you liked the book. A book review is quite different from a book summary and requires higher level thinking. Your objective in a book review is to analyze how effectively the author has made his or her arguments. While you will give a brief summary of the book, your primary focus will be on the author's thesis and use of evidence. You may not be an expert on the subject, but you should be able to read carefully enough to determine whether the author provided evidence to support her arguments.

When a professor assigns you a book to review, it is quite unlikely that the book will be a novel, which is just a made-up story. Instead, you will probably be reviewing a monograph, which is a scholarly book on a narrowly focused topic. Call this work a monograph or a book, but do not call it a novel.

In preparing to write the book review, read the book carefully. Take notes on the author's thesis, which will probably be found in the Introduction. The monograph's Introduction will also contain brief summaries of each chapter, and explain how these chapters support the book's thesis. As you read through the chapters, consider whether each provides enough evidence to support the book's thesis. Are there questions that you have as you read, or places where you wish the author had provided more explanation? Take notes as you go along.

At the start of your book review, provide the book's bibliographic information. For example:

Dropping out of Socialism: The Creation of Alternative Spheres in the Soviet Bloc. Edited by Juliane Furst and Josie McClellan. (Lanham, MD: Lexington Books, 2016. Pp. 352. Cloth, $116; Paper, $42.99.)

As you write your review, you should first summarize the book *briefly*, noting the author's thesis; in a five-page book review, this summary should take no more than one and a half pages. Next, describe the author's point of view and reasons for writing the book; check the book's foreword or preface for this information. Is the book part of a series? If so, include that information here, too.

Next, you will need to discuss the book's thesis. "When writing a book review, be sure that you are distinguishing between the book's subject matter and the book's thesis, or argument. Every book will have a main topic upon which it is focusing (a war, a revolution, an important social trend). The book's argument is the specific interpretation that the author is making of the book's main topic. For example, you are summarizing the main topic of a book if you say, 'This book discusses the reasons that the Russian Revolution occurred.' You are summarizing the main thesis, or argument, of the book if you say, 'This author argues that the Russian Revolution occurred due to the disintegration of loyalty to the imperial system at nearly all levels of Russian society.' This is an argument because it is the author's own interpretation of why this historical event occurred, based on his or her historical research, and because another book on the identical topic of the Russian Revolution could propose an entirely different, even contradictory, explanation for why the Revolution occurred."[1]

The heart of your book review will be an explanation of the arguments the author presents to support his/her thesis. Discuss the kinds of evidence and sources the author uses. Is the author relying on letters and diaries, newspaper articles, interviews, etc.? Does the author use primary or secondary sources? Do you find the evidence convincing? Explain why you do or do not find the author's evidence and arguments convincing, and explain whether or not the arguments and evidence adequately support the thesis. It may be that you find the author's thesis and evidence quite convincing, and that is fine. It may be that you have a few lingering questions; this is the place to express those questions. In a five-page book review, this section should be two to three pages in length.

Conclude your review with a final evaluation of the book. Do you think this is a book that is suitable for college classes, or for specialists only? Do you think it would appeal to a general audience? Do you think the book addresses a necessary topic or is the area of just minor importance? You can address one or more of these or similar questions in your final evaluation.

---

[1] Madigan Fichter, email to the author, May 24, 2020.

It is fine to use brief quotations from the book (providing page references for any quotations), but the review should be primarily in your words. It should not be a series of extended quotations from the book. If you do use quotations, you need to provide both quotation marks and a citation to the author's work. It is also fine to look at the reviews written by other historians after you have written your own, but this should be your work and your evaluation of the book, which your professor would not expect to be the work of a trained historian in the field of history covered by the book.

Annotated Bibliography

An annotated bibliography may be a complete assignment, or it may be one step in the process of writing a research paper. It is a bibliography in which you give a brief synopsis or summary of each source in the bibliography. As in a research paper, you will look for sources that will help you to answer a particular research question, such as books, journal articles, websites, and primary sources. You will then create a standard bibliography, though at the direction of your instructor you may have subcategories for the bibliography such as primary sources and secondary sources. The bibliographic entries should be arranged in alphabetical order by author's last name in each category and provide a full bibliographic citation. For each entry, you will then provide a brief synopsis of the work in question. Remember, as with the book review, you need to distinguish between the book's topic and the book's thesis. In the example below, the book's topic is addressed in the first sentence, while the third through fifth sentences address the book's thesis:

> Ulrich, Laurel Thatcher. *A Midwife's Tale: The Life of Martha Ballard Based on Her Diary, 1785-1812*. New York: Alfred A. Knopf, 1990.

In her Pulitzer Prize–winning study, Ulrich uses the diary of Martha Ballard to better understand women's lives and society on the Maine frontier in the early years of the Republic. Embracing the ordinariness of Ballard's diary entries ("Cloudy part of the day . . . I have been at home. Dolly warpt a piece for Mrs. Pollard of 39 yards," reads part of one entry), Ulrich uses the diary to elucidate the role of women in frontier society. Because her daughters were at home, weaving and tending to cooking and cleaning during their teenage years, Ulrich argues, Ballard could increase her share of the midwifery cases in her community; she delivered hundreds of babies in her community and also nursed the sick. The money that Ballard and her daughters earned went toward providing the young women's dowries. Social histories of the early republic have typically focused on the dominant roles of husbands and fathers, but Ulrich demonstrates that creative use of primary sources can reveal a parallel economic and social community of wives and mothers.

Footnotes and Endnotes

As you write your paper, be sure to keep close track of the sources you use to write each paragraph or to make each new point, because an essential part of writing is citing your sources. Historians use the Chicago Style of citation, which is different from MLA or APA, and they use footnotes or endnotes, rather than in-text citation. On using footnotes or endnotes generally, see Kate Turabian, *A Manual for Writers*, or *The Chicago Manual*. Summaries are available on-line at: University of Wisconsin Chicago/Turabian documentation

There are two times when you need to provide citations:

1. When you use a direct quotation from another source. In this case, you must put quotation marks around the words you are quoting; you must quote exactly without changing the words (although you can use ellipses [. . .] to indicate if you drop words in the middle or end of the quote); and you must provide a citation identifying the source of the quote you are using.
2. When you borrow ideas or information from another author. In this case you do not have to use quotation marks, but you must still acknowledge that the ideas and the information are not your own by providing a citation to the source you used. And, yes, this means your papers will have a lot of citations.

You will create footnotes or endnotes to cite your sources; in either case, the format is the same. The only difference is whether the notes appear at the bottom of each page (footnotes) or at the end of the paper (endnotes). The following are examples of typical sources that you may need to footnote:

To footnote a book:

Name of the author (or editor), Underlined title of the book, the edition of the book (place of publication: name of publisher, date of publication), page number.

(If the author is unknown, start with the title. If the book is by an editor or a compiler, use ed. or comp. after the author's name. If there are more than two authors, put only the first author's name followed by et al. [and others].)

To footnote an article in a book collection:

Name of the author. "Title of the article in quotation marks," in Underlined title of the book, ed. editor's name, the edition of the book (place of publication: name of publisher, date of publication), page numbers (e.g., 33–57).

To footnote a journal article:

Name of the author. "Title of the article in quotation marks," Underlined title of the journal, journal volume number (year of publication), page numbers (e.g., 112–143).

To footnote an online journal article or journal article from a database:

Name of the author. "Article title." Underlined Journal title. Journal volume number (year of publication), page numbers if available. URL and access date.

For example:

Cynthia A. Kierner. "Hospitality, Sociability, and Gender in the Southern Colonies." Journal of Southern History. Vol. 62, No. 3 (1996), 449–480. http://jstor.org/ (accessed May 7, 2020).

To footnote a newspaper:

Name of the author. "Title of the article in quotation marks," Underlined title of the newspaper, date of the newspaper, section of the newspaper if applicable, edition of the newspaper if applicable.

To footnote an unpublished thesis or dissertation:

Name of the author. "Title of the thesis," (MA Thesis or PhD diss.: institution, year), page number.

To footnote a television or radio show:

"The episode title if there is one," The series or show title underlined, the name of the producer or director, the running time, the name of the production company, the date the show was produced, and the streaming service where you saw the show.
"Forever Free," The Civil War, produced by Ken Burns, 11 hours, PBS Video, 1990, PBS.

To footnote a website:

The author or organization that created the website, "the title of the website in quotation marks" <the URL in angle brackets> (the date you accessed the website in parentheses).

To footnote a primary source document:
Letter:

Name of the person who wrote the letter to Name of the person who received the letter, date of letter, Collection of letters (if known), Archive (if known) <web address> (date you retrieved the information).

For example:

M.D. Clayton to her Aunt, May 8, 1840, Franklin County Personal Papers, Eve of War, Valley of the Shadow Archives <www.valley.vcdh.virginia.edu > (May 4, 2020).

Document:

Name of the person/organization who created the document, Title of document, date of document, Archive (if known) <web address> (date you retrieved the information).

For example:

John J. Crittenden, Amendments Posed in Congress, Dec. 18, 1860, Avalon Project at Yale Law School <http://www.yale.edu/lawweb/Avalon/Avalon.htm> (May 4, 2020).

Chicago Style Bibliographic Guidelines

The information found in a bibliography is the same as the information found in a footnote; only the format changes. List the sources in the bibliography alphabetically by author's last name.

Book:

> Author's last name, first name. Book title. Place of publication: publisher, date.

Journal Article:

> Name of author. "Article title." Journal title. Journal number (publication date), page numbers if available.

Online journal article or journal article from a database:

> Name of author. "Article title." Journal title. Journal number (publication date), page numbers if available. URL and access date:

For example:

> Girard, Philippe R. "Black Talleyrand: Toussaint Louverture's Diplomacy, 1798-1802." William and Mary Quarterly, 3d Ser., Vol. LXVI, No. 1 (2009), 87–124.
> Kierner, Cynthia A. "Hospitality, Sociability, and Gender in the Southern Colonies." Journal of Southern History. Vol. 62, No. 3 (1996), 449–480. http://jstor.org/ (accessed May 7, 2020).
> Watson, Harry L. Liberty and Power: The Politics of Jacksonian America. Rev. Ed. New York: Hill and Wang, 2006.

Website:

> The author or organization that created the website, "The title of the webpage in quotation marks," *The title of the website underlined or italicized*. The URL (the date you accessed the website in parentheses).

Government publication:

> The name of the city/state/country issuing the report. The author or issuing body. *Title of the document italicized or underlined*. The name of the author, editor, or compiler. The report number. The publisher if applicable. The date.

Online government publication:

> The author or issuing body. *Title of the document italicized or underlined*. Date. The URL (the date you accessed the website in parentheses).

Avoiding Plagiarism

Providing accurate citations is important because it is one step toward avoiding accusations of plagiarism. Universities take plagiarism seriously, and subject students to progressive sanctions for any form of cheating or plagiarism, including failing an assignment, failing a course, or dismissal from the university.

The first step to avoiding plagiarism is to cite the information you use. If you use someone else's ideas and information you are responsible for providing a citation, just as you are responsible if you use someone else's exact words. In other words, even if you are not copying a document word for word, you still need to cite it.

A second step to avoiding plagiarism is to put information into your own words. This is where students often trip up; you do not mean to plagiarize, but you are not sure how far you have to go in rewriting information from a book to make it really "your own words." Here is an example.

Original Passage
The settlers knew that the task of colonization would not be easy, but they could scarcely have imagined the extremity of the hardships that awaited them. They reached Plymouth a little before Christmas, just as winter was settling in. Weakened by the long period of confinement and inadequate nourishment on shipboard, they soon enough found that their very survival was in question. Sickness swept through the entire company, and within six months nearly half of them were dead.

Unacceptable Paraphrase
The settlers knew that the task of colonization would not be easy, but they could hardly have imagined how hard it would be. They reached Plymouth just before December 25. Weakened by the long time aboard ship and by inadequate food, they soon found that their survival was in question. Sickness swept through the entire company, and within a few months nearly half had died.

(continued)

> **Acceptable Paraphrase**
> The combination of a difficult Atlantic crossing, a lack of food, and sickness proved fatal to scores of the Pilgrims who embarked for Plymouth in 1620. They had spent weeks aboard ship in their voyage from England, and the close quarters, lack of exercise, and inadequate food and water compromised their immune systems. Arriving in late December of 1620, they were unable to plant crops to feed themselves during the long winter months. By spring, just over half still survived.

In the unacceptable example, the format of the paragraph and the format of each sentence stayed the same; the author only changed some words. The acceptable paraphrase, on the other hand, uses some but not all of the information that was in the original source, rearranges the sentences, and adds in new information that was not in the original source.

Revising Your Paper

When you have written the first draft of your paper, it is best to set it aside for a few days before you proofread and start to revise. When you have become very familiar with your work, it is easy for your eyes to skip over words and sentences as you read; putting it aside for a while will allow you to give it a fresh look.

As you revise, keep in mind a list of points to double-check:

1. Do you have a clear thesis in your introduction?
2. Do you provide evidence to support your thesis?
3. Do you refer back to the same thesis in your conclusion?
4. Is your paper organized in a logical fashion?
    a. Does each paragraph focus on one central point, rather than including lots of unconnected topics in a single paragraph? Does each paragraph have a topic sentence?
    b. Do you develop your argument and set out evidence in a logical way?
    c. Does your paper address events in a chronological fashion? For example, if you are discussing Germany's sweep across Europe in the early years of World War II, it would make no sense to discuss the invasion of France (in 1940) before addressing the blitzkrieg against Poland (in 1939).
5. Do you keep your paper focused on the topic while eliminating irrelevant information? If your paper is about China's Cultural Revolution, you should not go off on a tangent about Sun Yat-sen's education.
6. Are you referring to people in the paper by last names, rather than first names? Write about Roosevelt, not Franklin, or about Bolivar, not Simon.
7. Have you hidden your paper's scaffolding? Rather than write "in this paper, I am going to . . ." just state what it is you are arguing.
8. Have you used the past tense of verbs because most of the subjects and events you are writing about occurred in the past? *Lincoln was president during the Civil War—not Lincoln is president.*

9. Have you used the active voice, not the passive voice of verbs? *The US Cavalry slaughtered the Sioux* is more powerful than *The Sioux were slaughtered by the US Cavalry.* Passive voice is also not as informative: *"The North and South were reunited in 1865"* omits any mention of how this reunification was accomplished, namely, by Civil War.
10. Have you avoided contractions and abbreviations in your writing? Avoid words like *won't, IDK, govt, they've*. Avoid slang and profanity as well; history papers require more formal speech.
11. Remember to proofread for mistakes in spelling, misused words, sentence fragments, and errors in punctuation.

If you have time, try to give the paper to a friend or family member to read, and ask the person to mark any places where s/he has questions while reading; these may indicate spots where you need to include more information.

If your professor asks to see an outline or a rough draft before you submit the final draft, try to hand in as complete a version as possible. A professor cannot say much about a paper that just promises "text to come," but may be able to provide a lot of helpful advice on a paper that is largely complete.

Check if your university has a writing or tutoring center where you can bring your paper so that someone else can take a second look at it; if the center has peer reviewers, you may even encounter a student who has taken the same class already and can give you tips to be successful in the course.

Chapter 8
Grammar and Mechanics

Introduction

Grammar and mechanics work together to make writing intelligible. Mechanics sets of rules for the English language that address issues such as: language structure, parts of speech, capitalization, spelling, and punctuation. Using grammar effectively helps clarify meaning for a reader. It helps to create academic voice and gives the author credibility.

Grammar and mechanics are issues that should be addressed during revision and editing of a work. The rules apply to academic writing in every discipline and in every form. These rules provide a basis for understanding that crosses boundaries of your major or your assignment. They should be applied to every writing assignment from response writing in ENGL 101 to capstone papers in senior seminar classes.

Sometimes, grammar and mechanics feel like the boring parts of writing, but they do not have to be. If you think of grammar and mechanics like vanilla ice cream, it might help. Vanilla ice cream can be delicious on its own, but when paired with different toppings, vanilla ice cream can be transformed. Grammar is like that. It is the plain basis of written communication. Content and style are like the toppings; they are what the writer adds, but they are consumable by the reader if poor grammar makes them difficult to comprehend.

Overview of Chapter:

I. Introduction
II. Objectives
III. Key Definitions
IV. Key Grammar Issues
    A. Sentence Boundary Errors
        1. Exercise 1
    B. Subject–Verb Agreement Errors
        1. Exercise 2
    C. Tense Agreement Errors
        1. Exercise 3
    D. Active and Passive Voice Errors
        1. Exercise 4
    E. Pronoun Agreement Errors
        1. Exercise 5
V. Culminating Exercise
    F. General Guidelines
    G. First page of Text
VI. MLA Style Guide is on the Way
VII. Summary

Objectives

In college writing, there are a few errors in grammar and mechanics that stand out as problematic for many students. The goal of this chapter is to review them and to provide exercises that allow you, as a student writer, to work with each concept. When you have reviewed the concepts of this chapter, you can then apply them to your own writing.

The issues on which this chapter will focus are:

1. Sentence Boundary Problems: run-ons, comma splices, fragments
2. Subject–Verb Agreement
3. Tense Agreement
4. Active/Passive Voice
5. Pronoun Agreement

The objectives of the chapter are:

1. Demonstrate knowledge of grammar/mechanics
2. Apply concepts of grammar/mechanics to individual sentences
3. Apply concepts of grammar/mechanics to revise a text

Key Definitions

Active Voice—occurs when the subject of the sentence is the doer of the action or state of being of the verb in the sentence. It is the preferred voice for academic writing.

Agreement—occurs when two words match in gender and/or number. The concept applies to both pronoun/antecedent agreement and to subject–verb agreement.

Antecedent—word(s) to which a pronoun refers.

Comma Splice—a sentence boundary error that occurs when two more independent clauses are joined by a comma instead of ending punctuation, a semicolon, or a coordinating conjunction.

Fragment—an incomplete sentence or dependent clause without connection to an independent clause.

Passive Voice—occurs when the object of the sentence is the doer of the action or state of being of the verb in the sentence. It should be avoided in academic writing.

Noun—a word referring to a person place or thing.

Pronoun—a word that takes the place of a noun; pronouns can be subject or object pronouns, singular or plural or possessive.

Adjective—descriptive words within sentences that provide important details and necessary information to convey emotion and tone. Adjectives describe nouns.

Verbs—are words that denote actions and are the thing that explains what the subject matter of a sentence is doing.

Prepositions—are words that tell the reader where or when something is (on, in, behind, etc.).

Conjunctions—are words like "and" or "but" that help connect sentences together with the use of a comma. They can also connect concepts and clauses, or they can appear at the end of a list.

Interjections—are words like "yikes" or "wow" that are used to convey extreme emotion in a sentence.

Run On—a sentence boundary error that occurs when two or more independent clauses are merged without the use of ending punctuation, a semi-colon, or a coordinating conjunction.

Verb Tense—indicates the time in which an action has occurred. Present, past, and future are the most common verb tenses in the English language. Academic writing should use the present tense.

Subject–Verb Agreement—has to do with the idea that singular subjects are connected to singular verbs and plural subjects are connected to plural verbs. For example, *My Mother **is** a Lawyer* would be an example of correct, singular subject–verb agreement. *My parents **are** teachers* would be an example of a correct plural subject–verb agreement.

Usage—the correct application of a rule of grammar/mechanics.

Key Grammar Issues

Sentence Boundary Errors

Sentence boundary errors refer to any errors that either present a complete sentence as an incomplete sentence or fuse two or more complete sentences together. These errors most commonly include: fragments, comma splices, and run-ons. Each of these errors creates a problem in meaning for the reader. Correcting sentence boundary errors makes writing more understandable.

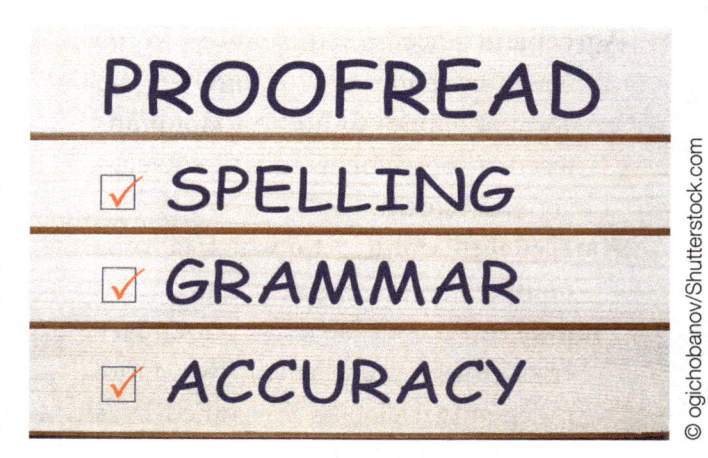

Examples of sentence boundary errors:

Fragment:
1. Until the problem of ozone depletion can be fully addressed.
2. And the economic burden placed on those in the lower classes is even worse.

Comma Splice:
1. The traffic problems were not easily solved with red light cameras, the fines were also rarely paid on time.
2. Some people claimed to have heard the explosion from miles away, others could smell the fire.

Run-on:
1. General education gives students a chance to be exposed to many branches of the humanities, natural and social sciences it provides a broad base of knowledge regardless of a student's major.
2. The election was contentious many people that fraud occurred.

Exercise 1

Directions: Identify the sentence boundary problem in each example. Then revise each example to provide correct sentence structures.

1. The women marched in protest, many brought their children _____
2. It was a wonderful novel the student enjoyed reading it very much_____
3. Whereas some felt the measures were too extreme _____
4. Hamilton served with General Washington handling his correspondence he longed for a battalion of his own to lead _____
5. Sherman Alexie is considered a great Spokane-Coeur d'Alene-American novelist many still feel Native American writers are underrepresented in the American canon _____
6. But the new academic supports helped student to succeed _____

Subject–Verb Agreement Errors

The subject and verb of a sentence must agree in number. Number refers to whether a word is singular (one) or plural (more than one). Collective subjects which refer to multiple people or objects, but act a singular entity, take singular verbs.

Examples of Subject–Verb Agreement Errors:

1. Dr. Alverez keep his class materials all in his Canvas course shell. (The verb should be "keeps.")
2. Students looks in Modules each week to find assignment, video content, and ancillary readings. (The verb should be "look.")
3. The class continue asking questions that is answered in the syllabus. (The verbs should be "continues" and "are.")

> **Exercise 2**
> Correct the subject–verb agreement errors in the following sentences.
>
> 1. Some argue that too much screen time are bad for young children. _____
> 2. Others state that screen time offer educational opportunities that previous generations did not have. _____
> 3. Some parents watches all online content with their children. _____
> 4. A preschool teacher offer a workshop on online safety for children. _____
> 5. Children enjoys learning online in a safe environment. _____

Tense Agreement Errors

Within a body of writing, such an as academic essay, research paper, literature review, or case study, it is important that verb tenses are consistent throughout the work. Verb tense refers to the time indicated by the verb in sentence. The basic verb tenses in the English language are present, past, and future. When a writer switches tenses in a discussion that has not changed time period, the switch confused the reader and compromises meaning. Tense agreement can also be referred to as tense consistency.

Example of Tense Agreement Errors:

It was a scalding hot July in Philadelphia, 1776. In a small room, in the fledgling colony of Pennsylvania, a group of white male land owners gather to write a document to send to back to King George. They had been demanding greater rights and freedoms from the British monarchy for some time and now are ready to assert themselves. In a document written mostly by Thomas Jefferson, and signed by fifty-six men, the American colonies declare independence from the British empire. Today, we celebrate July 4 as the founding of our nation.

> **Exercise 3**
> Using the above paragraph, practice correcting tense agreement errors. Rewrite the paragraph using the tense most appropriate to the content. Only consider changing tense if the time indicated in the sentence has changed.

Active/Passive Voice Errors

Voice refers to the style or personality of a piece of writing. When creating work for an academic audience, the voice of the piece must be credible and confident. The voice must convey accurate content and well-informed opinion, when required. Academic writing should employ active voice, meaning the subject of each sentence is the doer of the action of the sentence. Passive voice is the opposite of active voice and makes the object of the sentence the doer of the action. It tends to make writing less confident, less credible, and wordier.

Examples of Active and Passive Voice:

Active Voice: Plant workers protested the dumping of chemicals in the river last weekend.
Passive Voice: Last weekend, the dumping of chemicals in the river was protested by plant workers.
Active Voice: Maria attended a workshop on the basics of vehicle maintenance.
Passive Voice: The workshop on the basics of vehicle maintenance was attended by Maria.

> **Exercise 4**
> Revise the following sentences, taking each from passive to active voice.
>
> 1. The Zoom meeting was hosted by our friend's sister, for her birthday.
> 2. The disruption in cell service was caused by the severe storm passing through our area.
> 3. Innovative methods were used by the teachers to engage their students during the pandemic.
> 4. The patient was asked by the nurse about his pain level.
> 5. The injury was caused by the skateboarder's fall from a failed 360.

Pronoun Agreement Errors

Pronoun agreement refers to the coordination of a pronoun to its antecedent. This agreement usually refers to consistency in gender and number of the pronoun to the antecedent. It is important to note that recently grammar rules have changed to be more inclusive with regard to gender. Although still not considered singular pronouns in all examples, "they/them" can be correctly used to refer to a singular individual whose gender is unknown, fluid, or non-binary.

Pronoun Agreement Examples:

1. Incorrect agreement: The governmental agencies worked together until it found a cohesive operational plan.

Correct agreement: The governmental agencies worked together until they found a cohesive operational plan.
2. Incorrect Agreement: The woman protesting held its sign high for all to read.
Correct Agreement: The woman protesting held her sign for all to read.
   Or
   The women protesting held their sign for all to read.

> **Exercise 5**
> Correct the following pronoun agreement errors by writing the correct pronoun at the end of the sentence.
>
> 1. The group of children were given the opportunity to express her feelings during group time with the school counselor. _____.
> 2. Many of the men involved opposed his employer's new child leave policy. _____
> 3. The storm is progressing on his expected track toward the coast. _____
> 4. Angela enjoys time with its pets. _____
> 5. Jason and Sergy were conducting an experiment his lab. _____

Culminating Exercise

Directions: The following paragraph contains errors from all areas of grammar/mechanics reviewed in this section. Revise the paragraph to correct all errors.

The history of musical theater begin with the vaudeville circuit musical review acts toured the country performing its acts for audiences from all walks of life. Some of the greatest vaudeville acts started sustained runs on Broadway. Eventually, audiences want sustained storylines, so book musical were developed. The combined complicated dramatic plots with orchestral scores. Outstanding vocals and choreography, they were loved by audiences. Today, the traditional musical conventions is being challenged. It is now using rock music, contemporary plot, inclusive characters, and immediately relevant themes to connect with their audience. Musical theater will continue to grow. And develop as an artform.

MLA Formatting:

For most of your English courses…

MLA Formatting Guidelines: (taken from https://owl.purdue.edu/owl/research_and_citation/mla_style/mla_formatting_and_style_guide/mla_general_format.html)

General Guidelines

- Type your paper on a computer and print it out on standard, white 8.5 × 11-inch paper.
- Double-space the text of your paper and use a legible font (e.g., Times New Roman). Whatever font you choose, MLA recommends that the regular and italics type styles contrast enough that they are each distinct from one another. The font size should be 12 pt.
- Leave only one space after periods or other punctuation marks (unless otherwise prompted by your instructor).
- Set the margins of your document to 1 inch on all sides.
- Indent the first line of each paragraph one half-inch from the left margin. MLA recommends that you use the "Tab" key as opposed to pushing the space bar five times.
- Create a header that numbers all pages consecutively in the upper right-hand corner, one-half inch from the top, and flush with the right margin. (Note: Your instructor may ask that you omit the number on your first page. Always follow your instructor's guidelines.)
- Use italics throughout your essay to indicate the titles of longer works and, only when absolutely necessary, provide emphasis.
- If you have any endnotes, include them on a separate page before your Works Cited page. Entitle the section Notes (centered, unformatted).

First page of text

- Do not make a title page for your paper unless specifically requested.
- In the upper-left-hand corner of the first page, list your name, your instructor's name, the course, and the date. Again, be sure to use double-spaced text.
- Double-space again and center the title. Do not underline, italicize, or place your title in quotation marks. Write the title in Title Case (standard capitalization; remember, conjunctions,

prepositions, and articles and determiners are not capitalized but verbs, nouns, pronouns, adverbs, adjectives are), not in ALL CAPITAL letters. For example, This "Is" "the" Title Case.
- Use quotation marks and/or italics when referring to other works in your title, just as you would in your text. For example: *Fear and Loathing in Las Vegas* as Morality Play; Human Weariness in "After Apple Picking."
- Double-space between the title and the first line of the text.
- Create a header in the upper-right-hand corner that includes your last name, followed by a space with a page number. Number all pages consecutively with Arabic numerals (1, 2, 3, 4, etc.), one-half inch from the top and flush with the right margin. (Note: Your instructor or other readers may ask that you omit the last name/page number header on your first page. Always follow instructor guidelines.)

MLA Style Guide is on the Way

Summary

Grammar, syntax, and citation formatting are essential components of college writing. Strong and accurate grammar brings credibility to writing and strengthens the writer's ability to convey accurate meaning. Clear and correct citations allow for readers to understand the research that you have done in order to back up your arguments and ideas. The editing process is the ideal time for writers to check the accuracy of their grammar and citations and correct any possible errors. While grammar and spell check function in word processing software is a good start, those programs frequently miss errors. Nothing works like the human eye, at least for now. Don't yet trust the software to do what is still, fundamentally, a human job. Spell-check is a complimentary process and is certainly not foolproof. It is important that each writer check their work themselves, reading word for word, to ensure accuracy of grammar and meaning. It takes more than giving your final version a once-over to be sure that your document is error-free, in terms of both spelling and grammar.

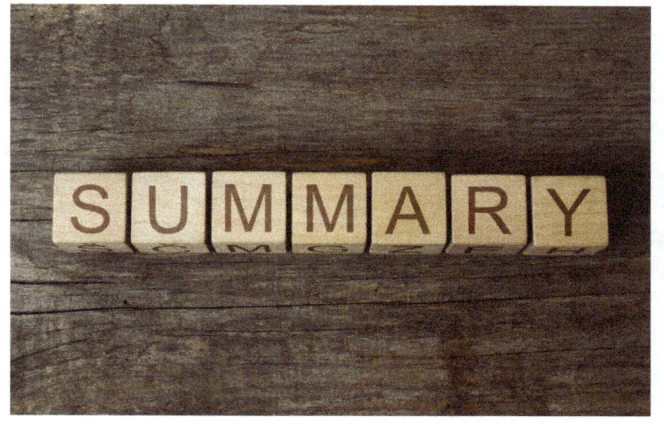

Chapter 9
Writing in the Digital World

Most college students engage in a variety of daily writing activities. Consider Gianna Z., a student at a university much like your own. Over the course of a day, Gianna texts her cousins about online shopping and has an argument over text with her boyfriend about sports movies. For school, she completes online teaching evaluations, outlines and sends exam questions to her Anatomy professor, and writes a reflection paper about fake news. Gianna texts her friend about the Spanish final; then, on Instagram, she posts three stories, including one about taking pictures on the beach, which leads to typing a workout schedule. Finally, she texts her mom about groceries and handwrites a bucket list for the summer.

Gianna's narrative reveals that she spends a lot of time writing in a variety of genres, formats, and for different audiences. Nearly all of her writing utilizes **digital technologies**, which are electronic tools, systems, and devices that process data; examples include mobile phones, computers, the internet, apps, and social media.[1] Like Gianna, most college students use electronic devices to write assignments for classes, emails to professors, texts to friends and family, and posts and comments on social media.

Digital technologies have become an integral part of our lives that have profoundly impacted how we write. Many people complain that texting and social media are negatively affecting students' ability to write and think.[2] Some believe that studying **digital technologies** in school is ridiculous. However, others argue that even a simple meme is a complex rhetorical task worthy of study and that digital technologies have enabled students to write thoughtful, complex pieces that can make a difference in the world.[3] This chapter takes the latter view and aims to provide a deeper understanding of writing in the digital world so that you can become a more purposeful, empowered, and ethical participant.

---

[1] https://www.education.vic.gov.au/school/teachers/teachingresources/digital/Pages/teach.aspx
[2] https://www.theatlantic.com/magazine/archive/2008/07/is-google-making-us-stupid/306868/
[3] https://news.stanford.edu/news/2009/october12/lunsford-writing-research-101209.html

Overview of Chapter:

I. Unique Features of Digital Writing
II. Rhetoric in Digital Spaces
    A. WHY and WHEN: Exigence and Kairos
    B. WHO: Audience
    C. WHERE: Digital Media
    D. WHAT: The Message
III. Final Exercise: Digital Media Project

I Unique Features of Digital Writing

Writing is undeniably shaped by the vast array of **digital technologies** available. Some unique features of digital writing include:

- *Connectivity and Interactivity.* **Digital technologies** facilitate real-time interaction between writers and readers. Our devices enable us to write anytime and anywhere, to anyone who is also digitally connected. We can be notified when we are texted or a new item is posted on social media, and as we scroll through Instagram or surf the internet, we are encouraged to click on ads, leave comments, and "like" posts. Thus, digital technologies promote networking in the broadest sense: bringing people together to exchange ideas and opinions.
- *Spreadability/Virality.* Due to the interconnected networks of digital media, messages can spread more quickly and widely than what is possible through print. Many digital compositions can be characterized as **memes**, which are pieces of culture that spread, evolve, and adapt like genes.[4] Digital technologies enable **memes** to propagate rapidly throughout social networks—in other words, go "viral." An example of a viral meme is the "OK Boomer" phrase that has prompted online debates, news stories, songs, and even merch.
- *Volume and Diversity.* **Digital technologies** have exponentially increased the number of writers and writing. Anyone can publish online, creating an ever-growing mass of information and opinions. All kinds of writing are being produced and published online and on social media, covering a limitless array of topics.
- *Multimodality.* In discussing digital "writing," we cannot consider only language. A digital composition can also include images, emojis, videos, links, and hashtags, which create a unique and complex vernacular.
- *Change.* **Digital technologies** are changing constantly. New technologies are being created all the time, and existing technologies are also evolving rapidly.

The sheer abundance and non-stop development of digital writing makes it challenging to analyze; however, there are many tools that we can use to make sense of it all. Counterintuitively, to analyze digital writing we need to go back to basics, to long before there were computers or cell phones.

---

[4] https://www.sciencefriday.com/articles/the-origin-of-the-word-meme/

II Rhetoric in Digital Spaces

In the fourth century BCE, Aristotle, a Greek philosopher, developed the theory of **rhetoric**, which he defined as "the ability to see what is possibly persuasive in every given case."[5] According to Aristotle, the rhetorician, while unable to convince everyone, will nonetheless consider and employ strategies, such as rhetorical appeals, to persuade the audience. Successful bloggers, businesses and nonprofits, celebrities, and influencers all use rhetorical appeals in their online and digital writing, in a sense making them modern-day rhetoricians.

A. *Rhetorical Appeals.* Aristotle identified three rhetorical appeals: ethos (credibility), pathos (emotion), and logos (logic). These appeals can be used to compose and analyze any content, from ancient to digital, but the appeals will have unique features in each context.
   a. **Ethos** refers to the credibility, reputation, and authority of the writer. An individual or a brand can use many tactics to build their ethos online, such as providing credentials, avoiding clickbait, and citing sources. On social media, the number of followers can help one's ethos (which has led to the practice of buying followers). Authenticity is a popular approach, as audiences often want someone who seems "real" rather than overly staged or edited. However, too much realness can backfire, as the audience may attack an individual or brand for controversial statements or actions. The loss of ethos online is associated with being "canceled."
   b. **Pathos** refers to the strategy of evoking the audience's emotions, beliefs, and values to stimulate action. Happiness and fear are two powerful emotions that are exacerbated by digital technologies. For example, many advertisers use FOMO (fear of missing out) to push their products and services.[6]
   c. **Logos** refers to the logical arguments of the piece, the evidence presented to back up claims. Appeals to logic include expert opinion, statistics, data, and facts. The personal testimonial is a popular form of evidence online and on social media, as brands strive to get influencers to sponsor their products. Online surveys and reviews can provide quantitative and qualitative evidence to support claims.

> **Exercise:**
> - *Find a digital composition—such as a meme or social media post—and analyze its use of rhetorical appeals.*

B. *The Rhetorical Situation.* In the twentieth century, scholars such as Kenneth Burke built upon Aristotle's foundation to develop the **rhetorical situation**, a concept that explains the dynamic between the writer and audience, as well as the medium used to convey the message between the two. In simpler terms, the rhetorical situation can help us answer the fundamental questions of **why, when, who, where, how,** and **what.** Whether you are writing an essay for class or

---

[5] https://plato.stanford.edu/entries/aristotle-rhetoric/#4.1
[6] https://optinmonster.com/fomo-marketing-examples-to-boost-sales/

an Instagram post, you must consider **why** you are writing it, **when** you are writing it, **who** you hope to reach, **where** you are presenting the message, and **how** you choose to write the message (**what**). Each of these components, and how they relate to digital technologies, will be addressed in the following sections.

1. WHY and WHEN: Exigence and Kairos

> **Exercises:**
> - *What are some of the exigencies that have moved you to write?*
> - *Give an example of when you created exigence; how did you employ ethos, pathos, and logos?*
> - *Identify an online or digital composition that you think exhibits strong kairos and explain why.*

You may have expected to start with the question of what you are writing because when we read and write, we tend to focus on what the passage is saying. The message, however, is shaped by the other, often-overlooked elements in the rhetorical situation. So, while our first inclination when reading or writing a piece is to figure out its meaning, we should consider all the factors that shape its content. The questions of why and when are essential for understanding what has been written.

There is always a reason **why** we write, something that moves us to express ourselves. In rhetoric, the impetus for writing is called **exigence**—Latin for *demand*—which refers to "an issue, problem, or situation that causes or prompts someone to write or speak."[7]

Exigence is everywhere. In a class, assignments and prompts given by the teacher create the exigence for writing. For example, you may be asked to summarize a reading, analyze an article, or defend an argument. Even if you are not particularly interested in the topic, the desire to pass the class gives you the motivation to write, especially as the due date draws nearer! Outside of class, your everyday interactions and experiences create **exigence.** You may have a good or bad experience at a restaurant and leave a review on Google or Yelp. When someone emails or texts you, you are often moved to reply. Perhaps you watch a TikTok video and feel the need to comment, or you read a Tweet that makes you want to respond or retweet.

Digital technologies have amplified exigence, as the average person is inundated with demands to write—emails from professors and bosses, texts from family members and friends, posts and @'s on social media, and surveys from businesses, to name a few. In exposing us to many perspectives and information, the internet and social media have multiplied our reasons for writing, and the interactive nature of these platforms gives us the means and motivation to enter countless conversations. However, with so much out there, choosing what to write about can be challenging.

On the flip side, we also find ourselves in the position of trying to create exigence, that is, motivating others to do something. For instance, you may want your professor to extend a deadline, your parent to send you money, or a friend to help you with homework. If you have a social media account, you want people to engage with your content by liking, following, and commenting. To effectively

---
[7]https://www.thoughtco.com/exigence-rhetoric-term-1690688

make these demands, you will employ the rhetorical appeals of ethos, pathos, and logos—though how you do so will largely depend on your audience (see next section on "who").

An issue related to exigence is **when** to write about something. The timeliness or relevance of a message at a particular moment was called **kairos** by Aristotle. Timing has always mattered, but digital technologies have magnified the importance of **kairos** because of the speed of communication. An article, Tweet, or post could be outdated in a few months or even weeks.

2. WHO: Audience

Why and when are related to who, in that once you have decided to write, you must consider who will read it—in other words, your audience. Audience is a crucial consideration for any writing task, whether your audience consists of one person (text message), a familiar group of people (Facebook group or group chat), or an unknown group (online article or blog post). You probably already have an awareness of this fact, as you unconsciously adapt to different audiences when you write. For example, an email to your professor would be composed differently than a text to your mom or a DM to a friend. While this may seem obvious, let's dig a bit deeper.

Familiar Audiences and Discourse Communities. A lot of the time your audience consists of people you know well. One way to think about audience is to consider **discourse communities**, groups of people who "share interests and ways of talking about them."[8] Everyone belongs to many **discourse communities**—such as family, neighborhood, school, sports teams, clubs, political party, interest-based groups—each of which communicates about certain topics in a particular ways, often employing inside jokes, allusions, and jargon that may not be understood by people outside of the group.

While **discourse communities** existed long before the creation of the internet and social media, digital technologies have affected how these groups are formed and how they communicate. While communities have traditionally been formed around geographic locations, many **discourse communities** now communicate digitally or online via group texts, Facebook groups, chatrooms, and social media. Plus, digital technologies have made it possible to form communities of people that interact online only and may never meet face to face. Members of marginalized groups, in particular, may be able to find a familiar and sympathetic audience online that they cannot always find in person.

Unfamiliar, Unintended, and Hostile Audiences. Unless you keep your social media accounts private, your online writing may reach audiences that you do not know and that you never expected to reach. The ability of digital pieces to spread rapidly and widely can be both an advantage and a problem. One can reach a large audience and create sympathy and solidarity among individuals who are separated geographically. However, spreadability also presents challenges, such as the lack of control over the audience and the potential for misunderstanding and conflict. The interactive nature of digital writing means that the audience is encouraged to respond, but one cannot always anticipate how they will react. It seems that every day we hear of a person or business that tweeted or posted something they regretted. Companies can find themselves in a PR nightmare while individuals may face criticism, trouble at work, and even harassment. (See "Ethics and Consequences" section in this chapter.)

---

[8]*Writing Moves: Composing in a Digital World*, ed. Eleanor Kutz, Denise Paster, and Christian J. Pulver, Southlake, TX: Fountain Head Press, 2018, 14.

> **Exercises:**
> - *Generate a list of discourse communities to which you belong. For each discourse community, identify the shared interests that bond the members, as well as the methods used to communicate.*
> - *Identify a controversial social media post and analyze it. What do you think was the intended message, and how/why did people interpret it differently?*

3. WHERE: Digital Media

When delivering a message, you must also think about where to place it. Before the rise of digital technologies, there were limited options for sharing and publishing your writing, for example, letters, books, articles, and other printed media. Now, because of digital technologies, we now have many more options for where to place our messages. Should it be in a private text to a friend, posted to Facebook, or shared with all your Instagram followers? Where depends heavily on who. The audience you want to reach should determine the forum or platform.

Every medium has tools and constraints that affect how a message can be communicated, and even the message itself. Consider the medium of Twitter. One of its tools is the hashtag, which allows users to categorize their Tweets and follow certain themes. For example, the #MeToo movement spread on Twitter via the viral hashtag that women used in their posts about their experiences of sexual harassment and assault. An obvious constraint of Twitter is its limit of 280 characters (doubled from 140 characters in 2017) that restricts the amount of information you can convey at once. The brevity of Twitter forces users to be concise, which can inspire pithy observations but can also make it challenging to have substantial conversations about issues.

In the digital world, "where" is much less restrictive than in the print world; digital writing can be recirculated throughout different media, including online articles, Pinterest, Facebook, Instagram, and even TV news. For instance, an article may be published in a print magazine, cited in an online article, referenced in a Tweet, and then reproduced on a Facebook page. The constant recirculation can make it difficult to trace "where" something first came from. Anything you write and share digitally may end up in places that you never expected. For example, the American College Health Association published a report about college student health in 2019.[9] The report was cited in an article published on the website *The Conversation*. Then, readers posted the article on Facebook and Twitter.

> **Exercises:**
> - *Choose one medium (text message, Facebook, Snapchat, YouTube, TikTok, etc.) and analyze the tools and constraints of it.*
> - *Find a popular meme or article and trace "where" it went, through different media.*

---

[9] https://www.acha.org/documents/ncha/NCHA-II_SPRING_2019_US_REFERENCE_GROUP_EXECUTIVE_SUMMARY.pdf

4. HOW

All of the previous topics relate to how you choose to compose your message, namely, the linguistic and nonlinguistic elements you use to convey your meaning.

a. Part I: Conventions, Style, and "Netiquette": Conventions refer to the expectations of a certain medium and audience. An academic research paper, for instance, is supposed to use Standard English, which has certain rules regarding capitalization, verb tenses, complete sentences, etc., as well as a citation style such as APA or MLA. Your audience, which consists of your teacher, and perhaps your classmates, expect that you will adhere to these rules. You may relate to Lindsay H. who admits, "I tend to use abbreviations and shortcuts when texting, so I have even caught myself in the past accidentally typing out 'u' in place of 'you' in a paper." When writing academic papers, make sure you proofread to catch these kinds of common errors.

For other media and audiences, however, the conventions may be different. While it may seem as though online writing has few or no rules, it is more accurate to say that the rules are different and often less well-defined. In some online and digital settings, Standard English is the default, such as the social media accounts for universities and businesses. In other communities, members will follow a different set of **conventions**. Of course, "writing" online does not only include language; using emojis, symbols, pictures, and video add to the flavor of writing and ideally facilitate understanding. For instance, you may use 😉 to indicate you are joking. Other emojis, like 💩, may be more ambiguous. **Discourse communities** can use these nonlinguistic elements in ways that are particular to members of the group.

All of these options give the writer the opportunity to create their own **style**—that special something that makes your writing recognizable to your friends and followers. You can craft your own **style** or styles for various audiences and media. You do not have to conform to what everyone else is doing, such as the tendency to ignore the rules of Standard English. As Laura D. states, "I'm the only one of my friends that doesn't really use any abbreviations or leave out punctuation over text, and I'm proud of that."

> **Exercise:**
> - Choose ONE medium and discourse community. Think about how you write in that forum. Give specific examples of how you use language and nonlinguistic elements like emojis.

At times, digital technologies may feel like a free-for-all, with everyone doing what they want with no regard for others. On the contrary, many are greatly concerned with establishing guiding principles to help make digital spaces safe and civil—in other words, determining **netiquette**.

"Netiquette" is a variation of the term "etiquette" that refers to the often-unspoken rules of appropriate behavior in certain situations. Emily Post was a famous American etiquette expert who wrote popular manuals during the early 20th century. She founded The Emily Post Institute that continues her legacy today by publishing etiquette guides that merge classic advice with updated guidance on how to navigate the digital world. While rules of etiquette used to be disseminated by a few experts, the rise of digital technologies have enabled anyone to participate in discussions of etiquette. A Google search of "netiquette" yields hundreds of thousands of results, as people weigh in on what they consider appropriate online behavior.

Netiquette depends on the audience and the medium. What is unacceptable in one discourse community may be fine in another. For example, WRITING IN ALL CAPS, which is considered bad manners for school or the workplace, may be considered acceptable and even essential for other online communities. Profanity, too, has a place and purpose for some communities.

Netiquette runs deeper than superficial manners. Emily Post emphasized, "Nothing is less important than which fork you use. Etiquette is the science of living. It embraces everything. It is ethics. It is honor." The ethical implications of digital writing are discussed in the next section.

> **Exercises:**
> - *Find a few netiquette guides online. What do they have in common? What's different?*
> - *Make your own netiquette guide for an online community to which you belong.*

b. **Part II: Ethics and Consequences** There have always been ethical issues surrounding writing, for example, plagiarism (stealing someone's words or ideas) and libel (publishing false statements about someone). The digital world, however, has created more challenges surrounding writing ethically.

Crediting Sources. While you probably know that you must cite sources in papers, you may not realize that it is equally important to give credit to your sources online and on social media. If you are writing a blog post, you should provide citations and hyperlinks to your online sources. When you retweet someone, you should give credit to the original tweet. If you repost an image on Instagram, you should include the creator's name or handle. Consult an online guide for how to credit someone in digital formats.

Getting Consent. Make sure you have permission to use someone else's words, ideas, or images. Not everything people write is intended for public consumption. For instance, someone may post something to a private account that they share only to their friends. If you want to reshare, ask them first. Also, do not assume that private text messages and snaps are meant to be shared with others.

Misinformation. Another issue with writing in the digital world is how easily misinformation can spread. Studies have shown that fake news spreads faster than real news on Twitter, not because of bots but because of people.[10] We all have a role to play to prevent the spread of misinformation. You should be careful about what you write and repost. Once misinformation is out there, it is incredibly difficult to retract. The spreadability and virality of digital writing means that information has a life of its own beyond the creator's control.

Bullying and Harassment. Digital spaces are unfortunately conducive to abusive behavior. A Pew Research Center study found that 41% of internet users had experienced online harassment.[11] Anonymity can make people feel detached from their actions. People write things online that they probably would not say in person because it is easier to dehumanize someone when they are only a screen name or Twitter handle. Many platforms are working to take

---
[10] https://www.sciencemag.org/news/2018/03/fake-news-spreads-faster-true-news-twitter-thanks-people-not-bots
[11] https://www.pewresearch.org/internet/2017/07/11/online-harassment-2017/

action against bullying and trolling, but we all have a part to play in making the internet a safer place.

Consequences. Miriam states that "you have to be careful what u put out on the internet because it can come back to you and sometimes you would have to face the consequences if it's something negative." Digital technologies can make us feel detached from the real world, but there can be very real consequences for what you write.

People have been sued and careers have been damaged by material posted online. Prospective employers may check out your online presence, which could affect your ability to get and keep a job. For example, Kaitlyn Walls was fired before she started her new job at a day care after she posted to Facebook: "I start my new job today, but I absolutely hate working at day care," and, "Lol, it's all good, I just really hate being around a lot of kids." Her post spread through a local Facebook page and came to the attention of her employers. Although Walls claims to have been "just venting," her case is a good reminder that nothing is truly private online.[12] Even if you set your accounts to private, whatever you post can still be shared.

Of course, online and digital writing can have positive consequences, too. People can get jobs through their social media networks and websites like LinkedIn. Important and accurate information can be spread widely and quickly. Creative and artistic works can find new audiences. Bonds can be formed between people regardless of geography. Collaboration can occur, leading to exciting new ideas. Digital technologies have made writing more democratic, enabling a greater range of people to write and publish for a wide audience.

> **Exercises :**
> - *Read the Pew Research study on online harassment: https://www.pewresearch.org/internet/2017/07/11/online-harassment-2017/.*
> - *What stands out to you from the study? What have your experiences been?*
> - *What are some positive experiences you have had using digital technologies?*

5. WHAT: The Message

Now, finally, we are going to address what you are writing about. As mentioned earlier, every topic under the sun can be found online. No matter your interest, digital technologies provide the means to write about it, publish your writing, and interact with readers.

Remember, though, the message does not exist in isolation; rather, it is shaped by the other factors discussed in this chapter. In other words, digital technologies have shaped not only how we write but also *what* we write about. Newspapers and news programs now regularly report on tweets, such as those written by the President of the United States. Topics like Tweets, influencers, TikToks, and Snapchats have infiltrated our conversations, articles, research papers, and even writing manuals.

There also has been a lot of writing focused on examining our relationship with these digital technologies, which is an issue we should all be thinking about. We need to try to understand the impact of these technologies instead of mindlessly using them. We need to see their potential but also their

---

[12] https://jezebel.com/woman-fired-before-first-day-of-job-for-facebook-post-a-1700628295

limitations and challenges. We are not passive observers of the digital world; we are active participants that shape the tools we use, and, as such, we need to take responsibility for how we use them.

Final Exercise: Digital Media Project

Think of an issue that you are passionate about and figure out how to best use digital technologies to spread your message. Consider how you can use the rhetorical appeals and the rhetorical situation. You can work in small groups on this project.

- Social media account dedicated to the issue: https://www.instagram.com/lilnativeboy/?hl=en
- Website or blog: https://www.thinkbeforeyoutypeinc.org/

After creating your digital media project, write a reflection paper in which you discuss how you employed the rhetorical appeals and rhetorical situation.